Couples with Intellectual Disabilities Talk about Living and Loving

D0175925

WOODBINE HOUSE • 1994

Cover design: Liz Wolf

Permission to reprint excerpts from the following is gratefully acknowledged:
Page 32: *Working* by Studs Terkel (1972). © New York: Pantheon Books, a division of
Random House, Inc.
Page 32: *Division Street* by Studs Terkel (1967). © Studs Terkel. With express permission
from the author.
Page 21–22: "What's Love Got to Do with It?" (1992) in *I Contact: Sexuality and People
with Developmental Disabilities* by Dave Hingsburger. Mountville, PA: Vida Publishing.
Page 187: "IN MY LIFE" by John Lennon and Paul McCartney © Copyright 1965
NORTHERN SONGS. Copyright renewed. All Rights Controlled and Administered by
MUSIC CORPORATION OF AMERICA, INC. Under License from NORTHERN SONGS
All Rights Reserved. International Copyright Secured. Used by Permission.
Page 192: *The Little Prince* (1943) by Antoine de Saint-Exupery. © 1943 and renewed
1971 by Harcourt Brace & Company, reprinted by permission of the publisher.
Page 2: *When All You've Ever Wanted Isn't Enough.* Copyright © by Kushner Enterprises,
Inc. Reprinted by permission of Simon & Schuster, Inc.

Library of Congress Cataloging-in-Publication Data:
Schwier, Karin Melberg.
   Couples with intellectual disabilities talk about living and loving / by Karin Melberg
Schwier.
      p.   cm.
   Includes bibliographical references.
   ISBN 0–933149–65–4 (paper) : $15.95
   1. Mentally handicapped—Marriage. 2. Man-woman relationships. 3. Mentally hand-
icapped—Sexual behavior. 4. Mentally handicapped—Interviews. I. Title.
HQ1041.S39 1994
306.7'087'4—dc20   94–6816
                                                                                    CIP

Contents

Acknowledgements

For Rick, a keeper

Warmest thanks to

Phil and Wendy Allen, Allen and Nadine Babcock, Mary Boychuk and Victor Pickard, Michael Creamer and Patsy Rinaldo, Bev Farrell and Trevor Waite, the Shane and Brenda Haddad family, Ellen Gajewski, the LaMarr and Kim Johnson family, Irene Lamb and Hoppy Sammons, Josh Lassiter and Debbie Herbert, Kaye McMurray and Gary Williams, the Ron and Hazel Neal family, Marianne Porter and James Richardson, Barry Smith, Wendy Smith, Brenda Thibault, Don Thibault;

The parents and staff who left us alone to talk, even though they were probably dying to know;

Co-executive producer Michael Nankin and particularly production assistant Mary Margaret Peters, Warner Brothers, *Life Goes On*, Burbank, California;

Sue Gates, Sue McKinnon, Jonathan Kieft and staff with the IHC (New Zealand Society for the Intellectually Handicapped, Inc.) respectively in Wellington and Auckland, New Zealand;

Susan Stokes, my editor at Woodbine House;

The Saskatchewan Association for Community Living, particularly its executive director Karen Rongve, for giving me a year's leave to pursue this project;

Author Studs Terkel, Chicago, Illinois, for his encouragement;

Author Robert Perske, Darien, Connecticut, as always;

And thank you with my love to Paul and Daphne Moxon, Matahuru, New Zealand, who didn't blink an eye, just opened their arms when I asked to come home again after 13 years.

"We need to belong intimately to a few people who are permanent elements in our lives. . . . A life without people . . . who belong to us, people who will be there for us, people who need us and whom we need in return, may be very rich in other things, but in human terms, it is no life at all . . . Just as our bodies have a need for air and food, our souls have a need to be connected to other people, not to be constantly surrounded by strangers. . . . One human being cannot be completely and authentically human without ongoing relationships with a few people. And they have to be people with whom we share our whole lives, not just a fraction of our time and ourselves. . . . All the complicated structures we spend so much time and energy creating are built on sand. Sooner or later, the wave will come along and knock down what we have worked so hard to build up. . . . Only the person who has somebody's hand to hold will be able to laugh."
—*Rabbi Harold Kushner*
When All You've Ever Wanted Isn't Enough

Foreword

Sometimes my husband and I feel like the odd offspring of Robert Fulghum and Dr. Ruth as we try to impart the meaning of life to our three children.

If only we could pry open the tops of their heads, dump in a copy of *Everything I Ever Needed to Know I Learned in Kindergarten,* a *Desiderata* poster, an appreciation for the arts, a smart money management guide, a love of animals, an ease of friend-making, an AIDS pamphlet, a good book about sexuality and sex, and a guarantee their chosen partner will last, snap the lid back on and hit the "save" key. We'd all live happily ever after.

Our eldest, Jim, is 20 years old. He knows how important it is to treat other people with courtesy and to begin sentences with "yes" instead of "no." We've drilled into him the necessity of a firm handshake. He understands "do unto others." He knows hitting is not allowed within the family; it is allowed if you are intimidated or touched by someone who doesn't stop when you tell them to do so. We've been careful to explain that although masturbation might feel good whenever the spirit moves you, it's not something for the grocery store or even the living room while the family watches television. It's private, something to be done "in your room." He's affectionate and doesn't hesitate, despite his teenage-ness, to express his feelings. He's got a sense of humor about sexuality; somebody says the word "peanuts," he is reminded of "penis" and it cracks him up. He and I have spent a lot of time learning the proper names for body parts; he was thrilled to report "Karin has a vagina! Dad has a penis!" when my husband's ex-wife called one Sunday. We've encouraged Jim's school to initiate a sex education class, using good social/sexuality training materials and an open, frank approach to the issues. We're supportive when he declares he'd like to get an apartment and "marry a wife."

But there's a painful question always lurking in our minds: will Jim ever have a happy and nurturing relationship, complete with a loving and satisfying sex life? What Jim does have, along with a handsome face, that warm sense of humor, and a tender, thoughtful concern for other people, is a list of deficits which stack the odds against such a relationship. He has a stutter and difficult-to-understand speech. He must wear two hearing aids. With those disabilities, many people manage to live interesting, sexually-fulfilled lives with a loving partner of their choice, but here's the extra kicker for Jim: he has Down syndrome.

Now almost at the end of his high school years, Jim has never had a girlfriend. He's never had a date. He's never had a sexual experience with a woman, or of any kind as far as we know. The issue of sexual abuse is another story (and Jim's avoided that dark epidemic), but the fact remains he's never had a romantic or sexual coupling of his choosing or desire. And the prospects don't look great.

> *One does not discover new lands*
> *without consenting to lose sight of the shore.*
> *— Andre Gide*

In one of our annual family Christmas letters to family and friends, we joked about our children growing up so fast. My husband, remembering what it was like when we were teenagers, quoted humorist Garrison Keillor, who said of his own youth, "Sex was an island across a vast body of water . . . and the church owned all the boats." Today our kids live in a marina. Jim has a boat, too. It leaks, though, and if we ever want him to even get a glimpse of that island, we've got to help him bail.

Though attitudes have changed dramatically since Jim was born in 1974, "intellectual disability" is not often listed among the top ten most desirable characteristics in a mate. Worse, society seems determined to conspire against people with intellectual disabilities and their chance for a loving sexual relationship with another person. Commonplace is the attitude that a relationship for someone with a disability, particularly one in which sexuality is physically expressed, is disgusting, repulsive, and somehow perverse. During the research for this book, a friend picked up a bibliography of books on sexuality and disability from my desk. "Aw, jeez," he said, grimacing and dropping the paper as though it were contaminated, "Why are you writing about *this* sort of stuff?"

The main reason is our son. We need to make his prospects a little better. For so long, we've been denying dignity and companionship, making life needlessly lonely for so many people already facing difficult challenges in their daily lives. Remember the elderly woman who got media attention for shooting her intellectually disabled son because she was afraid of dying and leaving him alone? We're denying people the chance to live interdependent lives with others who want to be close, who want to love. Why would we do that? Why would we work so hard to keep the network of people around a son or daughter with a intellectual disability so sparse that, when we die, there may be no one left?

Denial and dehumanization

Relationships in the human service system, where the emphasis is all too often on the "system" rather than the "human," are frequently, almost routinely ignored, punished, and actively discouraged. There are, of course, stellar examples where the opposite is true, but they are relatively few and far between. Where will Jim end up?

There are many illustrations of our denial that people with disabilities, particularly those with intellectual disabilities, are sexual beings. We forget that sexuality is so much more than merely sex; we overlook the need for companionship, conversation, trust, love, an appreciation for who we are as a male or female. It happens in families where parents are afraid of exploitation, are too uncomfortable to think about their child as anything but a child, or simply deny the sexuality of their son or daughter.

Even a friendship is seen by many parents as a dream that will never become a reality for their child. Sadly, many believe no one else would ever want to be with their son or daughter. That wall led one parent of a child with a disability to believe a phone call from a classmate to be nothing more than a cruel joke. The child telephoned her son, who was new to the class, to ask if he could come over after school one afternoon. The woman chastised the child for playing such a mean-spirited joke and slammed down the phone. Fortunately, the child told a teacher, who contacted the mother to assure her the boy's interest in her son was genuine. The mother broke down in tears.*

Even when we say we support the sexuality of and the right to relationships for people with disabilities, our actions don't always support our claims. In some of the very residential and vocational agencies offering "socio-sexual" training and support, situations like

---

*   *Hasbury, Dave. (1988). Frontier College, Toronto, Ontario. Personal conversations.*

the following occur, simple unto themselves, but profound in their dehumanization. Some have happy outcomes; most do not. (The names in these vignettes have been changed.)

> Dale, a quiet man in his 50s, who lived most of his life in an institution and who now lives in a group home, has become known to have a "problem" with masturbation. The agency has a written policy on sexuality, and he is to be trained to masturbate in the privacy of his room. Two young staff members purchase water pistols and keep them at the ready in case they "catch Dale in the act." When they do, they shoot him in the face with water until he stops and retreats to his room. If he is determined, they snap him with a wet dishtowel. At times when they see "precursor behavior," they show him a pistol or warn him with: "Dale, we're going to get the gun."

> A recognized couple have been seeing each other, mostly at the sheltered workshop where they both work, for years. John and Carol are in their mid-30s. An alarmed staff person "catches" them kissing and holding hands, so the two are separated and told if they are seen holding hands again at work at any time, they will be punished. Staff express concern that productivity will drop and say "if we let them do it, then everybody will want to do it."

> Heather, a young woman with a mild intellectual disability, and her two-year-old son Blaine moved into an approved home to learn parenting skills. The approved home operator and her new husband systematically took control of the child and eventually

literally locked Heather out of the house. Blaine, now four, calls the approved home operators "Mom" and "Dad." With support from an advocacy agency, Heather is in court to get her son back. When, in frustration, she spoke out of turn in court recently, the judge remarked to Heather's lawyer, "Well, there's certainly nothing wrong with her *mouth*, is there?"

Ralph, in his mid-40s, lived in an institution for many years. The unspoken procedure of the residents (segregated by sex) was to "sneak" to see a boyfriend or girlfriend if they wanted to meet without staff supervision. There were "secret hiding places," the location of which no one would divulge. Once, Ralph was caught on his return from meeting a woman. As his punishment, he was made to stand on a ladder with a toothbrush and scrub each individual hole in the ceiling tiles of the entire institution dining room.

Ray had lived for years in a segregated facility, so his only recourse for sex was with men. This did not necessarily mean Ray was homosexual, just that he had no access to women. When he moved into the community, he spoke of his desire to have a girlfriend. Staff introduced him to women, but these relationships would always end abruptly. Staff took this as a confirmation of their suspicions of Ray's homosexuality, and stopped encouraging his contact with women. Ray became lonely and despondent. Finally, a new staff person asked him why his relationships with women went so badly. "Oh, they go real good until we want to get in the bed, but then I'm scared." Why is that, the staff asked. "Because my dad told me women had teeth . . . down there . . . and if I ever put my penis in, they'd bite it off." It was the first time Ray had ever expressed his fears and, once assured his father had been mistaken, Ray was able to relax with women. He's now been with Sandy for nearly three years.

A societal repulsion, a damaging legacy

In our North American culture, we've been led to believe that physical beauty is a prerequisite for relationships, and that it's particularly crucial for sex. If people don't fit the Richard Gere-Cindy Crawford ideal, if we see bodies and movements different from those we are used to seeing, then we are uncomfortable envisioning the couple in bed. We're a society particularly disturbed with the idea of people who have physical and/or intellectual disabilities making love, expressing their sexual desires, possibly producing children or even being intimate with one another. Appreciating and understanding, even acknowledging, our sexuality is a measure of control we possess over our bodies and minds; perhaps that is a control we fear when in the hands of people we've deemed "defective."

We can thank extremists like Dr. Henry Goddard, who promoted eugenics theories in 1912, for instilling a dread of reproduction by people with disabilities. In his book *Minds Made Feeble: The Myth and Legacy of the Kallikaks,* author J. David Smith says this pseudo-scientist coined "moron," a term from a Greek word meaning foolish. He then set about warping the family tree of a New Jersey family to prove his theory that mental disability, and indeed most of society's ills, could be traced to the "bad seed" of "the feebleminded" and their descendants. Goddard advocated compulsory sterilization and segregated colonization to "remove these sores from our social life."

Eventually, Goddard's less-than-scientific theories crumbled under the weight of more scholarly work and contrary evidence, but the myth he created with such heated fervor has survived. His theories spread to Nazi Germany where compulsory sterilization led to what J. David Smith calls "the most comprehensive and vigorous eugenics program the world had ever known." People of the Jewish faith were not the only ones condemned to the gas chambers. People with disabilities, some diagnosed by a glance as "defective" by an overworked nurse or doctor, were sent to the "killing centers." Wolf Wolfensberger writes that ". . . among the estimated 300,000 mentally handicapped victims, perhaps 100,000 were mentally retarded."* Wolfensberger says that the euthanasia program was so successful that his 1963 visit to a German institution "revealed the presence of relatively few living units for mature adults because few mentally retarded adults were then to be found in Germany." While Hitler was certainly not the first to embrace eugenics efforts, he did so with frighteningly gleeful enthusiasm. In his pamphlet, "The Official Handbook for Schooling the Hitler Youth," he wrote: "Most of these congenitally diseased and less worthy persons are totally unsuited for living. . . ."

Hitler's actions seem diabolical today, but equally as frightening is how the roots of his ideas, and those of Goddard, still uncon-

---

*   *Wolfensberger, Wolf. (1981). "The Extermination of Handicapped People in World War II Germany,"* Mental Retardation, *19(1).*

sciously infect our way of thinking today. Countless babies born with Down syndrome and other disabilities have had their "feeding interrupted" and are allowed to starve, their lives deemed not worth living. Surgeries and other preventative interventions considered routine for non-disabled infants are sometimes withheld from those with disabling conditions.

Hitler's words echo in society's corridors even now. Smith's sobering research and writing of *Minds Made Feeble* led him to observe:

> "I have been reminded of, and made more sensitive to, how careful we must be in the sciences and in human service professions about the myths that we accept, foster, or even create. Myths have a way of becoming reality. Myths have a way of gathering force as they are passed along. They have a way of surviving the intent and lifetime of their creators."*

Despite the "Eve" decision in 1986 which made it illegal in Canada to perform non-therapeutic sterilizations without informed consent, Canadian lawyer Orville Endicott and many others are "certainly led to believe" the practice continues. Other forms of birth control, such as Depo Provera, are also used.

No matter what the procedure, however, sterilization causes the greatest concern, says Endicott, because of its "intrusiveness, irreversibility and sordid history" with people who are disabled. Dave Hingsburger, a noted Canadian sexuality counsellor and author,

---

*   *J. David Smith (1985).* Minds Made Feeble: The Myth and Legacy of the Kallikaks, *Austin, TX: PRO-ED, Inc., pp. 193-94.*

knows of parents who have taken their sons and daughters into the
United States, where sterilizations are easier to obtain. There, where
the precedent of "Eve" does not reach, parents pay for sterilizations.
"There are a lot of charlatans out there," he says. "I think sterilization is very widespread. It happens all the time, and many parents
are paying a lot of money." Hingsburger knows of parents who had
their young daughter clitorized because they were told it would
"redirect her energy." Hingsburger does not want to diminish the impact of the "Eve" case; Endicott agrees, adding, "Laws don't protect
people. People protect people." Self-advocates are beginning to
speak out. In Alberta, Canada, a woman sterilized while she lived in
Michener Centre, is suing the government. Several former residents
of Elwyn, an institution in Pennsylvania, who lived through the
hysteria of the eugenics era, are very angry about being sterilized
and have spoken publically. "There has been incredible damage to
self-esteem," says Hingsburger.

Today, social workers or even a next-door-neighbor can report
someone believed to be an "unfit" parent. People with intellectual
disabilities have had their children apprehended based on someone's
assumption that "*those* people" shouldn't be raising children. Of
course, the child's needs should be paramount, but the assumption
of parental incompetence is not always warranted. In many cases,
child protection proceedings move so slowly through the courts that
apprehended children become so attached to their new caregivers
that there is no turning back. Even if the parent wins back custody,
"the children have developed bonds that are very difficult and
damaging to break," says Endicott.

As people with intellectual disabilities struggle without guidance
or are punished for expressing their sexuality, we begin to realize
some of the problems we've created. At his counselling clinic in
Toronto, Hingsburger says most of the people he meets are "in

trouble because of their curiosity." Many people with intellectual disabilities are getting older and are not being educated about sexuality. "In human services, our most common response is to put someone, in effect, under house arrest. There may not be any charges, but the person is never let out of the group home without supervision. We lock people up rather than do any training. In human services, we want compliance. People should do what they're told, when they're told; if they don't, we put them on a behavior program, medication or we punish." Hingsburger urges parents of children with disabilities to begin sexuality training, which includes an appreciation for modesty and privacy, around the age of five.

A desperate loneliness

In Bernhard Stehle's extraordinary pictorial essay, *Incurably Romantic,* there is a particularly moving photograph of a young man, whose body is twisted by cerebral palsy, seated in his wheelchair. In his room in the institution, the man enthusiastically admires a poster taped to his wall of a beautiful and physically perfect Farrah Fawcett. It is a picture which is amusingly commonplace; a young man in his sexual prime admires a sex goddess created by the media. At the same time, it is a picture of sadness, of unfulfilled and—by today's mores—totally impractical desire. To say the chasm is wide between Farrah's tanned, swimsuited body and the young man in the wheelchair is classic understatement.

That chasm, and our relative inaction to bridge it, has led to lives of loneliness and isolation. As parents and service providers, we've asked for tolerance in society for people with disabilities and too often we've been grateful instead of insistent. Our sons and daughters cannot and must not be shielded from their sexuality, but taught how to embrace it. We must not settle for mere tolerance in society, but demand equal benefit. Any social/sexuality training course worth the registration fee will give an equal weight to self-esteem, confidence building and assertiveness training as it gives to body parts, reproduction, sexually transmitted diseases, and sex.

We preach friendships and community connections for people with disabilities. Yet we remove people from institutions without attention paid to friendships with people who also have disabilities. Ironically, in our efforts to integrate, we sometimes take away without replacing. The most important connection of all, a relationship with ourselves, must be nurtured. This does not mean a reticence about one's label as some would suggest. Rather, we must support people with disabilities to accept, appreciate, and celebrate themselves.

A 34-year-old woman I've known for many years, and with whom I get together for lunch now and then, called me at work one afternoon. She chatted happily for a while and then suddenly said, "I think I'm going to be in trouble."

"What do you mean, Shirley?"

"I ask two boys from school to come over. My parents weren't home. We were listening to tapes in my room. They took my clothes off."

My grip on the receiver was getting increasingly white-knuckled. But my voice surprised me; I sounded calm.

"What happened then?"

"They did it to me."

I wanted to be sure what she meant, and with calm questioning, I was eventually satisfied that when Shirley said "it," she really did mean "it." When I asked her if she wanted the men to do what they did, she said, "I don't know. I wanted them to like me." She told me her brother and sister-in-law knew and that she was going to the doctor for an examination. I told her she could call me back whenever she wanted to talk about it and she did, several times, over the next few weeks. She seemed okay; her biggest concern was that her parents probably wouldn't let her stay home alone anymore.

I found the whole episode disturbing and incredibly sad. This isolated woman felt her only hope of getting attention from men was to simply allow them to use her for sex. Sometimes when I look at my son, Shirley's words come back to haunt: "I just wanted them to like me."

Barriers to togetherness

One of the couples you'll meet in this book dreams of getting married one day. Mary wants to "take care of him" and Victor wants to "look after my little honey." But as much as they miss one another when apart, they can't afford to marry, or even move in together.

In the United States, when one or both partners are drawing government benefits, such as Supplemental Security Income, the couple can face a reduction in their benefits if they marry. For instance, in 1993 two people with intellectual disabilities could each draw up to $434 each month. If they legally married, the most they could draw between them was $652. In other countries, such as New Zealand, the main income support for people with an intellectual disability is the archaically-termed "Invalid's Benefit." As of 1993, the benefit for a single person was slightly over $664.00NZ per month (approximately $352.00 U.S.). However, if a couple married, the combined benefit was only $1104.00NZ ($585.12 U.S. or $292.56 each per month). For some people, a Disability Allowance could cover extra expenses faced because of the disability, but it was only $156.00NZ per month ($76.32 U.S.).

For nearly 900,000 Canadians with disabilities unemployed at
the time of the last census, financial support—or the loss of it—can
literally be a life or death consideration. If the choice is between
food and shelter or living with another human being, most people
will meet their most basic needs first. But the loneliness can be un-
bearable. Any time Mary and Victor speak of marriage, they talk
wistfully about "some day" and "a honeymoon in Hawaii maybe
when we get a little money saved up." In the meantime, they meet
for ice cream and coffee, and go for walks holding hands. He is 78,
she is 62. One wonders if "some day" will ever come for them.

There are other obstacles. Unlike in the U.S., in some Canadian
provinces no one is permitted to issue a marriage license to a couple
if it's suspected one or both lack the "capacity" to marry. A defini-
tion of capacity is uncertain, and interpretation is at the whim of the
issuer of licenses. In some cases, a legal guardian may have to give
permission. In some provinces, the couple must produce a letter
from a doctor testifying they understand what marriage is all about
(what is it all about, anyway?); in one province, a note from a
psychiatrist is required.

With these legal hoops, and a muddying of the already contaminated waters between intellectual disability and mental illness,
it often becomes hopeless for couples to marry. Many drift apart, or
are encouraged by family and staff to just forget one another. Others
simply remain as "boyfriend/girlfriend" for years, never fully recognized or respected as two adults who have chosen to spend their
lives together.

It was only 30 short years ago, that a man and woman caught
together in an institution had their heads shaved and were banished
to solitary confinement for weeks (Kempton, 1988). There were

routine sterilizations of women, even castrations of men. Only 30 years ago. . . .

A growing recognition

An unassuming weekly television series played no small part in an increased sensitivity about couples with disabilities. *Life Goes On,* the ABC series featuring the Thachers, a middle-class working family with three children (one with Down syndrome) gently opened eyes since its premiere in 1989. Its supporters called it a milestone in the efforts to bring attitudes about people with disabilities, and their families, out of the Dark Ages and into living rooms worldwide.

During the 1992 season, Corky Thacher and Amanda Swanson (Chris Burke and Andrea Friedman, actors who both have Down syndrome) elope. They simply decide to spend their lives together, find a judge and wed. Amanda's parents react with fear and panic, calling it an obvious "mistake" and try to have the union annulled in court. The anguished father, packing his daughter's belongings in her apartment, echoing voices of countless parents, staff, and guardians who only want to protect, tells Corky the marriage cannot be "because you're simply not capable."

Corky finds the capability, however, to speak up in court in defense of his marriage. "I know I'm not perfect and I can't do everything," he admits to his wife. "But I know how to do one thing. That's love you." When Amanda whispers that she'd like to go home with her husband, the judge swiftly reverses his initial decision to grant the annulment. If only life could imitate art more often.

Sometimes that art doesn't make its way onto the television screen. *Life Goes On* co-executive producer, Michael Nankin, admits to frustration with censors. Many storylines, particularly about the sexuality of Corky and Amanda, were abandoned—deemed too sensitive—and, Nankin asserts, "to tell them halfway would be a cheat. The honeymoon night for Corky and Amanda," he continues, "is quite intriguing and is really a story we never told. They just turn out the lights; we fade. But what does the scene look like on the wedding night for two totally sexually inexperienced people with (intellectual disabilities)? What about their first sexual encounter?" Despite the untold stories, Nankin is proud of what the series accomplished in its four-year run. "We told the story of Corky and Amanda in a charming way, with its joys and conflicts. . . . It's hard to find a sweet romance in this industry and we did it."

Indeed, the creators of *Life Goes On* brought a relationship between two people with intellectual disabilities into honest, open public view every week during the final segments. Broadcast restrictions aside, cast and crew were adjusting attitudes along with the audience. "I will admit there was a different approach among the staff to Chris and Andrea's love scenes than to Bill and Patti's (Bill Smitrovich and Patti Lupone, who played parents Drew and Libby Thacher)," says production assistant Mary Margaret Peters. "Everyone felt it was just more sensitive. It's different, but only because we're not used to seeing it."

In one of the final episodes, Corky awkwardly carries his bride across the threshold to their apartment over the Thachers' garage. They begin life together in a way many people with disabilities will never experience. Smiling, he leads her to the bed and as he pulls the shade and turns out the lights, hundreds of thousands of viewers come face to face with the sexuality of two people with Down syndrome.

And do you know what? It looks a whole lot like our own.

Minds are being opened with more urgency. In the fall of 1991, a sexuality and disability session packed them in at a conference in Ellensburg, Washington. The room was so crowded, people stood or sat in wheelchairs outside in the hallway, straining to listen.

Five or six people with disabilities and attendants faced the audience: Sharon Jodock-King and Alan King, both significantly physically handicapped by cerebral palsy (both use electronic reader boards to communicate) and two single men, Dennis Robertson and Jim Wicker, who also use wheelchairs. The session was moderated by James Watt, a sexuality counsellor, who told the crowd any question whatsoever about sexuality and, indeed, the sex lives of the panellists could be asked. Whether it would be answered would be at the discretion of each panel member. It was an amazing session, probably the most intense, personal, and controversial I've ever witnessed. In the audience were people with disabilities, friends, family members, human service supervisors, administrators, and direct service staff. People yelled, accused, blamed, laughed, cried. Many agreed to—and did—come back when the evening conference festivities were over to take up where the morning session had left off. People talked until well after 1 a.m.

The session was extraordinary because of this: people with disabilities so significant that they needed assistance with eating, communicating, washing, breathing, were—through interpreters and by hammering out words on communication boards—emphatically asserting their right and their desire to be, and be respected as, sexual.

For many, an attendant is their only tool for all the necessary activities of daily living. Some insisted an attendant, when asked, must place someone in bed for masturbation. For others, an attendant's job encompasses making sure a couple are positioned so they can make love in whatever way they are able. If the attendant refuses these tasks, many felt he or she should be fired.

Some staff in the audience agreed. Others were outraged; moral-
ly, they felt they should never be required to provide such intimate
assistance and could not be expected to do so. But, as many of the
people with disabilities simply pointed out, "You are hired as an ex-
tension of our bodies. If you are not willing or able to act in such a
way that allows us sexual expression, then who will?" Yet the
answers aren't always simple. What if an attendant is asked to physically assist with masturbation? What about assisting a couple in the
act of intercourse itself? At what point does the role of attendant
fade and that of sexual surrogate begin? How far is too far?

Some of the most eloquent statements came from a young man
with a disability and his attendant, both roughly the same age. The
attendant understood and respected his employer, someone with significant physical needs, and afforded him the dignity of his
sexuality. The disabled man explained, via an electronic reader
board, that he would ask to be taken to his room so he could mastur-
bate. The attendant would make sure the position was a comfortable
one, dim the lights, and quietly leave. After a time agreed upon in
advance, he'd return to quietly clean up and bring the man back to
continue with the activities of the day or evening. If the occasion
arose where his employer had a sexual partner, the same type of ar-
rangement would be followed. It was obvious the attendant and his
employer had a mutually respectful relationship. The attendant was
comfortable with his own sexuality and that of someone with a disability. He viewed as reasonable assistance the support necessary to
fulfil his employer's sexual desires. He saw it as part of his job in
support of daily living.

During that simple explanation, a man seated in front of me in the audience blushed, shuddered, and shook his head violently. He muttered to the person beside him that, "No way would any program ever force me to do *that* for anybody. That just ain't in my job description!" I looked at the back of that man's head and his red ears, then at the smiling attendant up at the front, who was leaning over to read a message on his employer's reader board.

With which person would I want our son Jim to live?
No contest.

An acknowledgement of the struggle

Dave Hingsburger, in his book *I Contact: Sexuality and People with Developmental Disabilities,* says the most difficult question any person with a disability ever asked him had nothing to do with sex. The most difficult question, he says, was "Dave, do you think it is okay for me to love?" He has allowed me to share his response:

> "I wish the answer could just be a simple yes. Yes, I believe it is okay for you to love. But can I give this answer? Can I sit in my comfortable office and tell a man I think it is okay for him to love another person? No, I cannot. When I first started, I found it easy to walk the moral high ground and tell people they had the right to be sexually whoever they chose as long as it was with a consenting adult. I felt the white knight on a crusade. Yet, I was never bloodied. I never faced battles in the trenches. Those people to whom I gave this correct but immature opinion paid the price. They were punished. They were separated. They put their heart on their sleeve and had it knock-

ed off. They believed and I deceived. This is unfair and unkind, and to this day, I grieve for not giving this question very serious thought.

"Do you think it's okay for me to love?"

So how, then, do I answer? How, then, do I advise? I cannot say "No" to this man simply because I know his staff and agency forbid sexual expression. I cannot ignore the fact that he said love. I cannot ignore that he is talking about sexual love. I cannot ignore the question. He looked at me sadly and expectantly. I had no easy answer. So I said,

"Yes, but it will take courage.

Courage because people will punish you. Systems will separate you and society will laugh at you.

Courage because churches may not marry you, laws may not allow you, and families may abandon you.

Courage because love does not grow easily in your world. Love upsets the delicate balance between us and you.

Courage because love makes us angry. Love makes us frightened when we see it. Love makes us see you differently.

Courage because you will need to hold on with all
the power in your grasp. You will need to persevere"
(pp. 105-107).*

Small first steps

Perhaps one of the most important things for families and advocates to remember is that initial connections for any of us aren't
usually based on extraordinary links. People meet, connect, continue, or fade away in everyone's life; the trick is to provide a
dynamic range of possibilities.

In the book *Friendships and Community Connections Between
People with and without Developmental Disabilities,* I contributed a
chapter called "Ordinary Miracles: Testimonies of Friendships." In
the following paragraph, I challenge the idea that any of us develop
and maintain friendships only because of clearly recognizable common interests and backgrounds.

> The "you two have so much in common and there-
> fore will be great friends" myth is a barrier that can
> drown the tender growth of ordinary friendships. As-
> sumptions and fears about people with disabilities
> and misconceptions about what they can offer have

---

* *Hingsburger, D. (1991).* I Contact: Sexuality and People with
Developmental Disabilities. *Mountville, PA: VIDA Publishing.*

> created isolation. But when the seeds of acquaintance
> are nurtured, even occasionally, gifts such as compas-
> sion, a sense of humor, a common interest, a hidden
> talent, the ability to listen, and other undiscovered
> wonders can flourish. . . . Having coffee, talking on
> the telephone, seeing a movie, including one another
> in celebrations, getting together to wash the car or
> the dog, or to go for an evening walk along the river
> are things of which friendships are made.*

Too often we've marched, despite good and honest intentions, from one extreme to another on the human services front. On one hand, we've actively denied relationships for people with dis- abilities, segregating people not only from the community at large but also men from women within that already devalued, isolated group. Or we justify the continuation of segregated, congregated set- tings for people with disabilities by declaring, "People find it easier to be friends if they have something in common. They're more com- fortable, happier with their own kind." The implication is, of course, people with disabilities are not of *our kind*.

On the other hand, as the more progressive among us realize the intrinsic value of connections and integration, we become so mechanical about structuring friendships that we run the risk of kill- ing all spontaneity, exploration, and surprise, the very elements of a satisfying relationship. "Friendship" becomes a goal to be checked

---

*   *Melberg Schwier, K. (1990). "Ordinary Miracles: Testimonies of Friendships" in* Friendships and Community Connections Between People with and without Disabilities. *A. N. Amado (ed). Baltimore, MD: Paul H. Brookes Publishing, p. 165.*

as a pass or fail on someone's chart at regular intervals. Who among us could live up to that kind of scrutiny?

As advocates, we must demand more than mere tolerance for our sons and daughters and friends in society. It is as important for our son Jim to *be* a friend as it is for him to have them. It's important for him to make some of the decisions about shopping, to take an active part in his everyday life, to learn the skills needed to interact with people as they spin by. Then, with any luck, Jim might have the courage to reach out when someone swirls by a little more slowly than the rest.

Traditionally, people with disabilities have been the recipients, beneficiaries, the "done-for" rather than the "do-for" someone else. Imagine life spent without ever giving; without ever being expected to be more than a recipient of someone else's "good deed" or paid service. We have ignored the basic human need to give something to another human being. One of my favorite authors, Robert Perske, writes:

> "As people talk to each other, persons with disabilities have been able to contribute their own unique richness to their friends and to the surrounding neighborhoods as well. . . . I believe that friendships with people who have disabilities can provide an explosion of fresh values and directions which this confused, misdirected world needs now as never before."*

---

*   *Perske, R. (1988).* Circles of Friends: People with Disabilities and Their Friends Enrich the Lives of One Another. *Nashville, TN: Abingdon Press.*

A more compassionate future

If a 50 percent divorce rate is any indication, half the population can't very well attest with any great certainty as to its wisdom on solid and lasting relationships. Domestic violence has never been more prevalent. Couples, for myriad reasons, drift apart, fall out of love or, equally as devastating, fall out of like with one another. Children are split as homes divide. Given our own track record, how many of us are in a position to knowingly predict the failings of a relationship between two people with a disability? In short, who are we to judge?

It would seem that human beings strive, some successfully and some miserably, for that Happily Ever After dream. We want to share it intimately with one person with whom we can be honest, open, and ourselves. We want to be secure in the knowledge that our partner will love us for our attractive qualities and will continue to do so despite our flaws and mistakes.

The supreme happiness of life
is the conviction that we are loved.
—Victor Hugo

The couples interviewed for this book are linked with a common thread, despite their differences in age, education, type of disability, nationality, and a host of other variables. Each one expressed a need for companionship, a friend, someone with whom to grow old. They wanted someone to like them for themselves, not someone paid to be there, not someone who will disappear in the next wave of staff turnover, someone other than parents and family.

Anyone can exist, anyone can go through the motions of life. But to share that life with another human being, to be cared for and loved, to be appreciated and valued is quite another thing. People no longer are content to be catalogued and shelved as "disabled." They want, and deserve, to be part of the whole. As Dennis Robertson, a self-advocate at the Washington conference, said, "I think people take one look at me and say in their minds: He won't ever have sex, so why talk about it and why get his hopes up? This makes me angry...because they could be wrong."

Learning to listen

When people with disabilities speak on their own behalf, often making statements at odds with parents and service providers, they are, ironically, accused of being "not really that handicapped." One parent complained bitterly after reading an article opposing sheltered workshops written by a well-known self-advocate. "I don't even think that guy's all that retarded," he scoffed. "And he says he's speaking for people with handicaps! Ha!" However, when that same parent learned that same self-advocate had a girlfriend who also had an intellectual disability, it confirmed his belief that "retarded people like to stick with their own." It only served to prove his conviction that, for instance, it was too idealistic for advocates to promote relationships outside the group home or employment opportunities outside the sheltered workshop. We all, it seems, hear what we want to hear.

Hearing what we want to hear, perhaps at the expense of what is said, led us to believe for many years that people with disabilities had nothing much to say. The rallying cry voiced by people in this book, some calmly and others with more defiance, will make some people uncomfortable. But to borrow the sentiment expressed by the people at the conference in Washington state: if we don't listen, then who will?

Change is difficult, and often humbling. Following the 1990 publication of my previous book, *Speakeasy: People with Mental Handicaps Talk about Their Lives in Institutions and in the Community,* a few grumblings were heard, not from the people who told their stories, but from those family members and staff who felt they had not been asked for their "side" or "version" of events. They are correct; they weren't asked. Professionals and, more recently families, have other forums, easier access to that which makes their voices heard. In *Speakeasy,* the "why" behind someone's placement in an institution was not relevant. Rather, the impact of such philanthropy, the lifetime effect of not only an intellectual disability, but of the segregation it created—and all in the voice of the person who had lived it—is paramount, and offers a look into the soul of the recipient of our "good works." Sometimes what we see isn't easy to accept.

Robert Perske directed me to the works of another individual interested in telling the stories of people whose voices are not ordinarily heard. In the course of several books, Studs Terkel masterfully and unobtrusively collected the oral histories of common people during the Depression, and of people at work and as they live in urban America. His narratives are rich with the agonies, pleasures, and observations of real people; their words are not glossy reproductions of politically correct responses. From them, we learn of life and their lives through no filter or fear of reprisal.

Neither filtered or interpreted are the words in this collection. A director of a large residential program said to me, following *Speakeasy*'s release, that one of the men interviewed "lived in fear that they would come to put him back in the institution." I'm still not sure if the statement was passed on as an interesting bit of information, or if it was meant as an accusation of irresponsible journalism. As someone with a intellectual disability not generally accustomed to having himself heard, perhaps the man felt having his say was worth the risk.

The people in this book continue to take that risk. Michael Creamer, 27, of Harrison, Ohio, placed his hands on his chest, over his heart, and struggled to find the right words when I asked him to tell me about his relationship. Michael and Patsy have known one another since they were children; the "buddies" grew into an exclusive couple over the years. With a supportive family behind him, Michael has difficulty realizing anyone would ever deny him the experience of being in love with a woman.

Closing his eyes, Michael says softly, somberly, "She makes me very happy most often. I know she cares for me. Very much. My heart feels good from her. I touch her. My heart is happy. She gives me a glad heart."

I hope we can give my son the courage to make his way, to be happy, hopefully hand in hand with a partner who'll appreciate and love his gentleness, his humor and his spirit. Someone who'll give our son a glad heart.

—K.M.S.
Saskatoon, Saskatchewan
February 1994

Author's Note

In the early stages of my career, I was a newspaper reporter and from the beginning my method of interviewing was to simply have a conversation. That is what I have continued to do as an advocacy writer as I gather the stories of people with disabilities, their families and friends. People whose lives are often dictated by charts and forms seem to relax without the pressure of a perceived pass or fail. So we just talk.

As people heard I was working on a book about couples, I received letters, notes, and phone calls from people who said, "You should really meet . . ." Some people in this book already I knew. Though I was interested in meeting "colorful" people, I was careful not to interview those who've already received a lot of attention. You won't find many people in this book who are recognized leaders in the self-advocacy movement; some have never heard of such a thing. Some are soft-spoken and reserved; some are more accustomed to making themselves heard. I was interested in a range of relationships in different countries; that's why you'll meet people who are just beginning to date, some who are married, some who live together, some with children and some who only dream of being together some day.

I'm only the vehicle for each couple to tell their story; I'm not doing the driving. The words you'll read in *Couples* are the words of those who spoke them. The interviews were gathered since *Speakeasy* was published in 1990, and the couples chosen for *Couples* came from interviews in Canada, the United States and New Zealand. Transcripts of the taped interviews were edited for length, and only occasionally were disjointed pieces fit together to maintain a theme in conversation. Some brief interviews were not edited at all. As you hold this book in your hands, I want you to feel as though you're sitting with Michael and Patsy in a Harrison, Ohio kitchen; with Allan and Nadine in a noisy Ellensburg, Washington pizza hang-out; under loblolly pine and dogwood trees with a giggling Josh and Debbie as they admire her ring in a Gainesville, Florida backyard; having afternoon tea with Irene and Hoppy in the sitting lounge of their Pukekohe, New Zealand flat; on the balcony of a Toronto highrise with Barry and Wendy Smith; in a Kentucky Fried Chicken booth in Assiniboia, Saskatchewan across from Mary and Victor. As you hold this book, look past the stereotypes. I want you to have a conversation.

(The tape recorder) can be used to capture the voice of a celebrity, whose answers are ever ready and flow through all the expected straits. I have yet to be astonished by one. It can be used to capture the thoughts of the non-celebrated—on the steps of a public housing project, in a frame bungalow, in a furnished apartment, in a parked car—and these "statistics" become persons, each one unique. I am constantly astonished.
—Studs Terkel
Working, *1972*

The question-and-answer technique may be of some value in determining favored detergents, toothpaste and deodorants, but not in the discovery of men and women.
—Studs Terkel
Division Street: America, *1967*

EARNEST BEGINNINGS

Friendship is a thing most necessary to life, since without friends no one would choose to live, though possessed of all other advantages.
—Aristotle

Kites rise highest against the wind, not with it.
—Sir Winston Churchill

Michael Creamer and Patsy Rinaldo

Harrison/Cincinnati, Ohio

M ichael Creamer's mother, Peggy, was a religious education teacher at Mother of Mercy High School in Cincinnati,
Ohio. In 1972, a "beautiful little girl called Patsy with long
blonde ringlets" started coming to the class. Immediately,
Michael and Patsy were "buddies." Because their children
had Down syndrome, the families were drawn together and
over the years watched as the buddies eventually became
boyfriend and girlfriend. Today Michael, 27, works a couple of
hours each day at the Senior Citizen's Center in Harrison,
Ohio, walking distance from the house where he lives with his
parents. After work, he watches a soap opera, works on his
baseball card collection or scrapbooks, or helps with yard
work. Every year, he vacations with his parents and the Rinal-
dos; sometimes he and his mother take trips on their own.

Soft-spoken Michael, born in Lawrenceburg, Indiana in
1966, quietly bore the more assertive Patsy's wrath when he
told her of a new friend he met square dancing. Patsy, 25, dis-
misses the new rival as "a floozie" and calls Michael "an idiot"
for taking any interest in her. Patsy, born in 1968, is unemployed, but helps her parents with housework and

yardwork at her home in Cincinnati. As the couple attempts to patch over the crack in their relationship, they sit at the Creamers' kitchen table and pore over photo albums of many combined family vacations. Patsy's parents have brought her from Cincinnati for an afternoon visit. After lunch, the adults pointedly disappear with coffee; the couple goes to Michael's basement bedroom to play music and dance. To Patsy, Michael is hers exclusively and her only close friend; Michael loves her, but wants to maintain other relationships. "I don't know how to explain to Patsy," he says. "She is, you know, so jealous, but I need my friends. You should have more than just one friend."

Michael: The best I like about Patsy is love. I take her out. Most often times we go to the movies. We like movies; that is Patsy's favorite one thing she likes. She is very pretty. She has not long hair. Very beautiful. She change her hair sometimes. She's pretty okay. She has a handle of me and she love me most often, but she is most often very *bossy*.

I like to do my own thing, too, and I have other friends, too, and Patsy not understand me. I just want to touch her and sometimes she is mad at me because I hurt her feelings. She does a good temper once, so I have to bring her back and talk about it, the jealous.

Sometimes I step out with my friends. I give you one guess: I like to go have a drink and we go to a bar or something like that. I like that. I like dancing a lot. I think it is important to let the one do their own thing and see friends. And not be bossy. I don't like that. I have a friend, he know me before. He is handicapped and I take care of him. He is not too far. I call him on the phone and he call me on the phone. He got a job serving lunch and he really like that. A lot.

I did too call Patsy on the phone. A lot. We talk about trip we been and movie we see most often. If I go on a trip with my mom, she ask me what I did. Lots of stuff. She just make me happy. She thinks of me, she thinks about me. She comes to my house sometimes for lunch with me. We go downstairs to my room and watch soaps or we look at pictures of trips. Sometimes we like to dance a lot. We know each other since we were little kids. A long time.

I put on my music and dance with her and touch her. She loves me. She's funny. She likes me so much and thinks I am very cute most often. When my dad did not feel too good, I cut the grass for him. My mom puts a garden most often, but she hates rabbits because they chew the garden down. I put dishes away and clear the table. I sweep. I do a good job.

I met this other girl. Lisa. At square dancing and she tell me she like boys. Patsy got mad. Lisa is a little boy crazy. I like girls very much. A lot. Because I am a normal man.

When Patsy and I go out on a date, we talk. We walk around the park most often. We ate together. We once were little kids. Little buddies together. Then we grow up and she makes me so proud. Her for me and she is happy. Patsy is a good personality. If someone tell me I can't have her, can't have a girlfriend, would explain most often love I feel for her, comes back to me from her. That's all. Only one thing bother me. She say to me to get away from my friends. I like my friends, so it is hard for me.

Patsy: (shrugs) I don't know what I like about Michael. He gave me this ring for anniversary. We know each other 20 years. He's sexy. He's nuts. We go dancin' sometimes. He blew it one time. He pick up a floozie. At a dance and I not like it. He's an idiot for that.

We go to movie. I like love movie (pushes at his arm). Quit starin' at me, I do! What I don't like about him he change clothes a lot. Ten, twenty times. But he buy me nice jewelery. I like to dress up. Look good. He is very serious. He tells jokes.

Michael: I remember first time I kiss her. I just watch her eyes and her face. I know she loves me. I kiss her just really long time ago when we were kids, but this different. Very different.

Patsy: (blushes) You are embarrassin' me.

Michael: I have my graduation at high school. They all cheer of me. And they cheer of Patsy at her high school for her. We each popular. They like us. I had fun in high school. They don't tease me. Some always call me retarded. I don't like it. That hurt me so I walk away. Ignore it. I don't know why people make me feel bad. I like math in high school. I went social studies and I like history. I learn about people on the oceans and I know a few things, but I forget. I am a writer. I write Patsy letters and I tell her I love her.

Patsy: (rolls her eyes) Stop it. You're makin' me sick. Michael gave me this ring. It for good luck, I guess, I don't remember. I don't want to get married. Not for long time. Sometime I want to kill him. When I get mad at him, I yell at him.

Michael: Sometimes I write to Patsy about her and how she make me happy. I call her darling and she like that. You have to look at your heart. Sometimes it break my heart when she is mad about my friends, but we talk. She talk to me about woman's feelings. Sometimes we go swimming. Patsy swim good.

My dad is married to my mother and my brother got married to a lady and divorce and my oldest sister get divorce. Being married it make me scared, nervous. I am happy like this. I don't know why people get divorce. They walk away. Bad stuff and they don't know why. They don't talk. Very sad.

I like Patsy. She is beautiful. I like her personality.

Patsy: He has a nice body. Good lookin'.

Michael: I like her style.

Patsy: (folds her arms) Oh, God . . .

Michael: Don't be embarrassed, darling.

Patsy: I like bowling. I got 141 and 140.

Michael: She is a very good bowler. She get five strike one time. We went to Disney World one time. Tell about that, Patsy.

Patsy: It was packed. Lots of people, crowded, can't move.

We like to go to dinner. I like Chinese food. I want to get married someday. If someone say we not supposed to fall in love, I just hit 'em. I say I do what I want. None of the business. I like George and Peggy, that's his mom and dad. I like his mustache. He says he shave it off. I tell him "Don't be a idiot." We kiss at home. At home is okay. Outside on the street is gross.

Michael: Patsy is proud of me and I understand her. She is special for me.

Patsy: (slaps his arm) Don't embarrass me. You're an idiot. I buy him a belt and a tie for his birthday. We went to Bahamas long time ago. That was fun. We like square dancin'. It's hard to do, but I like it. My dress, his tie match.

Michael: I like kids. My brother has a kid. He's five already. Alex. I am Uncle Michael. And I am a great uncle to Michelle's niece. I got two sisters and one brother and one nephew. And three niece. I like kids very much. We play and I look after them. They come to my house and I watch them play. I say "Don't get hurt. Be careful. Always calm down. No bully. That's not nice."

Patsy: I don't want to have kids. Just don't want to. Maybe when I am old. Too much work. They are pain in the neck. I like to have more fun.

Michael: My parents give us privacy. We go down in my room downstairs. They give us time alone. By ourselves. We watch movie together. We go for walk in park. We eat.

Patsy: He hold my hand when we walk.

Michael: She miss me when I go on a trip. I always buy something for her. A present.

Patsy: Yeah, right. You're sick. Cut it out.

Michael: I make macaroni and cheese. Bake beans. In the microwave. I done it myself before.

Patsy: I cook everything. I'm a good cook. Okay, I cook chicken. Bake potatoes. Steaks. Everything. I am not lazy to do it.

He is not too old for me. Sexy. That is what I like. I am not sexy. I eat too much sometime and get fat. We are friends. He is my boyfriend. For my birthday, we got a big limo. In Cincinnati. A man drove us around for three hours. We went to a park; it was muddy and snowin'. Sometime I give Michael a present, a picture of me. Sometimes we fight. But we make up. I kiss him. Give him big, big hug.

Michael: (nods) We make up good. We talk. I kiss her and just bring her back. Sometime she get mad so I talk about it. Just like that.

Patsy: (frowns) Sometime people tease us. They call me names. I don't like it. I punch 'em. I get upset.

Michael: (rubs her shoulder) You have to calm down yourself, Patsy. I will take care of you.

Patsy: Yeah, right. He gots lots of bowling trophies. Sometime we make a fire in the fireplace and we sit and talk. We play Nintendo. He got a exercise bike and I need it! I eat too much.

Michael: I watch my weight. I'm on a diet. I got a flat stomach. I did too have the flu once and Patsy take care of me. She did. When she is sick, I care for her.

Patsy: Yeah, right. I will die. I know it. Why don't you shave? I don't like a beard.

Michael: I did shave. I can't help it, my face, Patsy. You like it. Remember what you call me, Patsy? I call her darling. What you call me? Think hard.

Patsy: (smirks) Sexy. I call you sexy.

Michael: I call her darling. She is so hot. That is very best thing. She is pretty fun. Important for me, I like you the most, Patsy. But I like other friends, too.

Patsy: That is rude. I like you, too. You are all right. But sometimes you are idiot.

Michael: (softly) I will explain it like this. Patsy make me very happy inside me, in my heart most often. My heart feels good from her. I touch her. My heart is happy. She gives me a glad heart. That's it.

Kaye McMurray and Gary Williams

Christchurch, New Zealand

*I*n the kitchen, a stout young woman with her long black hair pulled back from her wide face in a ponytail, bobs tea bags in cups of hot water and smiles shyly. She carries the cups to "our lounge," a small, rather stark room in her Christchurch group home, decorated with color photographs tapod to thc wall. A small kitchen table in the center of the room is covered with an embroidered cloth, and she places the tea, milk, and sugar carefully in the center. Kaye McMurray's smile broadens as she hears Gary Williams' wheelchair whine its way down the corridor. He enters, also smiling, offering a hand as the chair lurches to a stop. Gary, 42, and Kaye, 22, are recognized by their three flatmates and staff as a couple. "This is our private place," she explains. "The staff said we could have this room to have our privacy so this is where we talk when it's nobody's business unless we ask them in." The group home is operated by the IHC (The New Zealand Society for the Intellectually Handicapped, Inc.).

She smooths back her straight bangs. "I am Maori," she declares proudly. "Gary is pakeha."* His thin body clenches and relaxes as he manages his cup of tea. He fights his way through bursts of words, muscles uncooperative because of cerebral palsy, but determination to have his say makes him persevere. As he talks, Kaye gazes at him with a small smile, occasionally clarifying or expanding, sometimes touching his hand. "If people are ignorant," he says, "we just don't take any notice of them, right, Kaye?"

The couple plan to marry one day when they have saved enough money. He works in the local tax department; she works at the Halifax New Brighton Marae** in Christchurch.

Kaye: They had a cooking class for some of them who would like to try flatting*** so we met each other, Gary and me. After awhile, we would go out to a restaurant for a meal or we'd have our own tea here when all the others had gone out for the evening. Sometimes we'd have tea, you know, fish and chips on our own. We'd even make a pudding or some biscuits even, what's it called? Fudge. I'm a really good cook. I'm musical talented, too, and I try to communicate with people, even when they aren't that neighborly.

I love Gary quite a bit. He's wonderful. He's very loving and caring. He's nice and very polite. He's just excellent. He's never

---

*   White.

**   *Maori ceremonial gathering place.*

****Apartment living.*

bossy or demanding; he's not like any of the other boys I used to go with. If he ever gets angry, he says let's talk. What I hope we are doing in the future is have a counsellor, sort of have a marriage counsellor and me and Gary will go and see her and understand things so me and Gary can stay together. For the rest of our lives, I reckon.

There are people who sometimes stare at us, but me and Gary just take no notice. I think they are very ignorant and Gary gets angry and we're just not going to put up with that sort of thing, we reckon. It makes a lot of pressure and hurts our feelings. Most people are very good to us.

We've been together a few months now. The IHC staff have encouraged us to be together and we've been sleeping together and they never stop us. Some of the relieving staff* take a bit of time to get used to us putting ourselves in sexuality positions.

Gary: One staff ask me does she sleep in my room? When Kaye first said she wanted to move into my room and sleep together and finally I was thinking at the same time, here goes, righty-o, let's do it! Kaye is very sweet and kind; that's all there is to it.

Kaye: I help him into bed. Well, we get used to help each other get into bed. I put him on the walker, get him out of the wheelchair and actually then we put the walker against the bed and it's all nice and easily. He holds onto and pushes up to the pillow and I tuck him in!

---

*   *On call or part-time staff.*

Gary: I was just thinkin' that if we just take it step by step, we'll be right. I was just thinkin', if Kaye doesn't mind that I tell you, loving is natural, you know. I'm quite happy with it and with Kaye.

Kaye: (smiles) Gary and I have been talkin' about this that one day in the future since we've been talkin' about it that in the future we will marry.

Gary: We've been in Christchurch for a long time and it would be good to see what's happening elsewhere.

Kaye: Like Canada. Or Germany. What we might have to do is save up our money for three years and use half and go to America or someplace. We're scared of some people who tease us and give us a fright and who are ignorant people and we're a bit scared of that, but I will stand by Gary.

Gary: (reaches for his tea) And I just says to Kaye I says the other night when I was just thinkin', I wouldn't part from her. She wouldn't let me go with anyone else now anyways.

Kaye: When I was at a party one night, I was dancin' and we got to know each other. By the way he was talkin' to me, I could tell he was really nice. I could understand him, you know, how he talks and I was just tickled pink.

Gary: Like I was tellin' Kaye, I was just thinkin' that we take things step by step. I'm not the type to rush things. There are people who criticize, but I'm not takin' any notice of them, I'm not. Not takin' any notice a'tall. They talk about me in a wheelchair, but it's not what you look like, is it then?

Kaye: (nods) That's exactly right.

Gary: We'll stay together as long as she's happy. I worked at several different places. I worked at the tax department and I did a bit of gardening and tidying up. I enjoy the outdoors.

Kaye: We need to think about several things before we get married, like making the right decisions and doing things the mature way and not rushing into it. We almost feel like we're married now.

I would wear for my wedding sort of a 1970s or '60s or '50s or sort of a country and western hat. White and burgundy stockings, lace, country and western boots, bustle, stuff like that, a horse and cart to ride around Christchurch. He'd wear country and western gear, too. I'd ask Tawahai Wawatai to be my best man. He's our staff. That's a Maori name. My real parents are Maori, but my adopted parents are pakeha, just like Gary. I'm an all around New Zealand Maori. I love my culture. I was always determined to practice and practice my Maori so I can speak properly in Maori, not like the pakeha way to say Maori words. I get very angry when I see the Maoris like me getting cut down on TV. I am proud to be Maori and I care about my Maori people. My tribe is Tainui tribe from Nelson. Maybe instead of country and western, we could have a Maori wedding. That would be at the marae. I'd like to find out more about it for me and Gary.

Gary: I'm actually musical meself so I really enjoy Kaye because she is very musical. One thing I have to talk with Kaye about. I was just thinkin' I would like to have more time to meself.

Kaye: (frowns, leans forward) You'd like more time for yourself?

Gary: Yes, sometimes.

Kaye: You have lots of time to yourself when I help you in the loo, on the toilet.

Gary: (nods) I want to be with Kaye almost all the time, but there are times when I'd like to have for meself. But Kaye and I are happy, but sometimes I'd like to be just by meself.

Kaye: We had a hangi for my 21st birthday. That's where the Maori people, we cook the food underground, wrapped in leaves. It's very healthy and good for you.
    Me and Gary, we never fight. Never.

Gary: If we disagree, we just sort it out immediately between us.

Kaye: (points to Gary, then herself) We talk about it immediately. We have a room here in the house that's set aside for us and when we go in there, the staff and others know we want our privacy. If we need some help, we will ask the staff to help us sort it out. But we ask. When we have disagreements, Gary never gets angry, just frustrated and he cries a little bit.

Gary: I see Kaye for who she is and she takes me for what I am. When it's frustrating is sometimes when Kaye's made up her mind and I've made up my mind and we stick to it. I haven't made up me mind yet about how to ask her to get married. I'm just doin' my own thing and trying to keep working. I don't get much enjoyment out of workin'. Not much money. I see Kaye at night time.

Kaye: I work at New Brighton and we do things like packaging chocolates, hand creams, soaps, key holders. Gary comes down on Wednesdays and he works.

Gary: I like to go there on Wednesdays. Better than being stuck up in the tax department. You just make the most of it, you know. I'm welcome over at Kaye's work anytime, aren't I, Kaye? I don't get much money. I do cook, I do. Most times, I like it. We take turns. I make short cake and . . .

Kaye: . . . roasts, pork, steaks, potatoes, kumara.* He boils and mashes them. They're pretty good.

Gary: (rubs his forehead, shrugs) I haven't done much cookin' though lately, have I, Kaye? Kaye thinks I'm gettin' a bit lazy, she does!

Kaye: (laughs) No, you're not! You're not lazy a'tall!
We'd like to have kids one day, but half our own and half adopted.

Gary: I wouldn't mind. I wouldn't mind havin' kids. I wouldn't mind bein' happy.

---

* *Native New Zealand sweet potato.*

Kaye: (speaks rapidly) Things come up in me mind about children bein' abused and terrible things happening to them. We'd like to take the pain away for them and take them and give them a new life. I would teach them to say no to strangers and if someone ever did anything horrible to my little boy or little girl, I would be angry at the person who did it. Some things people do to children make me sick. I don't like people smackin' little children. I lived in Braemer Hospital in Nelson for Disabled and Crippled Children's Society.

Gary: Like that lady on TV in Christchurch, on the news like. That had her baby taken. I was watchin' the news and she had her baby taken out of the bed at the hospital.

Kaye: I would teach a child not to touch things like stoves and ovens, things that could hurt them. I wouldn't buy them guns or things like Terminator dolls. I like Cabbage Kids and good toys. I would keep those things away from kids and help them grow out nice. I would teach them to come and tell us when something was wrong. I would be a caring person.

Gary: I was just thinkin' I just can't believe it to see some parents the way they treat their kids and have them on the street when they're supposed to be sleepin'. It makes me very sad, it does.

Kaye: If I took the kids over to my mother's, I would give her a list of all the things she could do and the things she couldn't do to them. She shouldn't let them touch medicine and things like that. My mother is a loving, caring mother but when she would sort of smack me, I would get very angry and I wouldn't let her smack my children.

Gary: (anxiously) I been thinkin' that they've been criticizing me and I've been patient, haven't I, Kaye? But I don't like it when people criticize other people. I don't like it one bit and I'm not takin' any notice of it. I just won't put up with it.

Kaye: (sits up straight) I'm not takin' any notice of it either. We're not handicapped. We don't like that word. We're intellectually disabled and just because we're a bit different doesn't mean we should be treated differently. We don't want to be taken for advantage or betrayed. We're equal to anyone else.

I would say no and make an objection to an operation so I couldn't have kids. That's something for us to decide. Me, I decide. If I'm comfortable with it, then maybe. But I decide. Me and Gary.

Gary: I was just thinkin' if we're goin' to get married, we might as well do it as soon as possible. I know when Kaye was away for three weeks, it wasn't much fun. I didn't like it one bit when she was gone. She's got her life and I've got mine, but being apart so long, it was a bit much. If we did get married, then we could move to a new place and when she had to go away, I could go with her. Isn't that right, Kaye?

Kaye: Too right, Gary.

Josh Lassiter and Debbie Herbert

High Springs/Gainesville, Florida

$\mathcal{T}$hey sit together on the couch, thighs touching; they inter-mittently giggle, kiss, interrupt, and correct each other during the interview, which is also attended by Debbie's mother, Jean, sister, Nicole, and Josh's parents, Linda and Chuck. Josh Lassiter, 19, of High Springs, Florida and Debbie Herbert, 18, of Gainesville, Florida have known each other since they were toddlers in an early intervention program. Their first offi-cial date was in 1989 when Josh's mother chauffeured them to a movie, *Bill and Ted's Excellent Adventure.* (Linda had to sit alone at the back of the theatre.) The two attend the same classes at Sidney Lanier School, a training center. Josh, born in 1974, is in a work experience program at Alachua General Hospital; Debbie works at Wal-Mart Department Store. Despite her brief infidelity with Joe McIntyre of The New Kids on the Block (he blew her a kiss at a concert), the couple declares emphatically, "We are in love."

Born in 1974 with a defective heart (one now deteriorating rapidly), Debbie was never expected to live beyond her first birthday. Her lips tinged blue, she explains how she must stay out of the hot Florida sun, mustn't walk too far or get over-tired. For a time, Debbie's mother was hesitant about the couple's deepening relationship. If Debbie should die, she worried, it would be too devastating for Josh. But for her 18th birthday, Josh saved his money to buy Debbie a "promise ring."

Josh: I was born on March 25 on my birthday. I 19 now. I work at Alachua Hospital; that's Debbie's hospital where she goes when she's sick. I do stuff there and, um, put trash in the trash cans and clean and stuff. I wear a shirt, a red one.

Debbie and me do have known each other for a long time. A long time. Debbie and me go to same preschool.

I like her cause she nice and she pretty and she is a cute little sweetie (pinches her cheek) and she is my girlfriend now. On my birthday I was 13 and I ask my mom and dad for money. So I could take Debbie on a date.

Debbie: (makes raspberry noise)

Josh: Um. I be nice to her and, um . . .

Debbie: What are you talking for?

Josh: Debbie. It's my turn to talk.

Well, um, Debbie loves me now and she's my girl.

Debbie: Wrong. (giggles)

Josh: Debbie. Please.

Debbie: He had a girlfriend.

Josh: Debbie. Please. Um, my old girlfriend, she is black. She have crutches. Her name is Flora. Debbie hate that, so, you know how it goes.

Debbie: He's cool. He's nice. We been goin' out, um . . . we fight a lot. He starts it.

Josh: No. Her.

Debbie: Him. (Both giggle)

Josh: We don't fight about nothin'. The last time we fight at my house on New Year's Day. . . .

Debbie: Josh. It's my turn.

Josh: Come on, go ahead.

Debbie: I like when he gets crazy. He is silly. Um . . . we go see movie.

Josh: Debbie, what you wanna see?

Debbie: I wanna go see, what's that movie, Nicole? (Her sister suggests *Sandlot*.)

Yeah! That's it. I wanna see it. We got popcorn. A big thing of popcorn. He buy it.

Josh: I do. I buy it. With my money. We go outta eat, too. We have our favorite place. Whaddaya call it, um, McDonald's.

Debbie: Yeah, McDonald's. We like McDonald's.

Josh: Oh, yeah, we like dancing. Dancing, yeah. We like it a lot. I think that's on the street by our school. We go to same school, me and Debbie. Sidney Lanier.

Debbie: Sidney Lanier.

Josh: Debbie. That's what I said. We in the same class. She is good student. She is very smart. Sometime for, you know, punishment, they don't let us sit together. For lunch, they don't let us sit together. I am sad. We not graduate yet, so we have to wait. We be 21 when we graduate.

Debbie: He 19. I'm a 18.

Josh: The last time we going out, Jean, that's Debbie's mom, take Debbie and me out. My mom, then my turn, I go with my mom and take Debbie out.

Debbie: Or your dad.

Josh: Or my dad.

My mom sits way in the back and me and Debbie sit way in the front and we, um, hold hands. That way it's just me and Debbie. By ourselves. Not my mom. Alone, and we, um, we get our hands on the popcorn.

Debbie: (giggles)

Josh: We don't go out every week. But lots of times we do. We talk on the phone every day. We be boyfriend and girlfriend for a *long* time. We are love and we go to high school and graduate and get marry some day.

Debbie: (rolls her eyes) PU-lease! Every single day he call me and say "Hi" and I say "Hi" and we talk. Sometimes I say, "Sorry, I have to go" and I hang up. (Parents interject: "It's a good thing we don't have to pay for local calls. They've talked to each other for up to six hours at a time." They call each other before they go to sleep and often before they go to school in the morning. Usually, the latter involves Josh trying to persuade Debbie to wear a dress.)

Josh: I won't going to marry her yet. But we will. Then we are husband and wife. She is my wife, too.

Debbie: Wrong.

Josh: You are.

Debbie: Wrong.

Josh: I say you are.

Debbie: I had other boyfriend. Josh, don't look at me like that.

Josh: Go ahead. Tell. It's okay.

Debbie: Well, I been goin' out with him. He's cute. And we been goin' out. And, um . . . (Nicole and the parents take interest; when Jean asks for his name, Debbie covers her face and giggles)

Um, his name is Joe McIntyre.

Josh: Oh, Debbie! Not him again!

Debbie: Yes! I went to a New Kids on the Block concert. In Orlando. Me and my mom. I was hopin' to get back stage pass so I could give him my phone number so he might call me. But, um, he was singin' on the stage and he blew me a kiss (sighs). After that, we come home. Then I got sick.

Nicole has a boyfriend. She been goin' out, too. I met somebody else, too. He's a kinda cute and he hold my hand, but I tell him to stop. In school.

Josh: (puts his hands on his hips) Debbie. Where?

Debbie: What?

Josh: Where? Where did he try to hold your hand?

Debbie: In the restroom.

Josh: Oh. Okay.

Debbie: Then me and him broke up and I go out with another cute boy. . . .

Josh: Debbie. Who?

Debbie: Josh. Can I tell the story? So, um, this cute boy his name is Josh Lassiter!

Josh: (hugs her) Yahoo! That's me!

Debbie: Okay. You can talk now.

Josh: See, my grannie, my mom's mother, you know, is getting a divorce. So. I don't want Debbie goin' like that. And she tell me, "Come on, Josh, I have to go, like outta town" and I say "Don't go leave on me, Debbie." If she go, that's it.

Debbie: That's it, he means we breakin' up.

Josh: No, it's not, Debbie. Um, but anyways. I guess she have to go someplace. I guess I am jealous.

Debbie: No, you're not.

Josh: Yeah, I do, too!

Debbie: Do you think I seein' someone else like you?

Josh: No.

Debbie: Well, okay then. That's a point.

Josh: We not get divorce. When we do get married, we move to a new house.

Debbie: PU-lease!

Josh: Around here somewhere (points to Jean's living room). Sometimes I think we live with Jean (Debbie's mother raises her eyebrows). Maybe we get a house by ourselves. Me and Debbie do our laundry and get food ready and fix dinner and stuff. I do cookin' at home. And Debbie, too. I make grill cheese sandwich. I try fix pizza and stuff like that, but the bread it burn.

Debbie: I cook. Chicken . . .

Josh: Oooo, that's good.

Debbie: Brownies.

Josh: (licks his lips) Woooo, that's good!

Debbie: Um. That's it.

Josh: Mom and me make brownies. At home. We know how to shop for groceries, me and Debbie.

Debbie: No, we don't!

Josh: Well, we learn to do it. All the money I get for my job . . .

Debbie: And my money from Wal-Mart. I make $200.

Josh: Whoa, Debbie! You rich!

Debbie: At Wal-Mart, um, I put things out. Hang 'em up. And I think that's it. I have a jacket (points to her lapel). Here is my tag with my name on it. I put my paycheck in the bank. Not all of it. I spend some.

(Quietly) I can't walk too far. Or get too much hot sun. I have heart problem. I go to hospital lots of times. One time Mom took me to the hospital and they put me on IV. There's something wrong with my heart. I don't know really. My mom knows (pats Josh's leg). He worry about me when I go to the hospital.

Josh: (takes her hand) I worry about her, too. I think she is ill cause a long time she is sick like this. I get upset sometime when she is sick cause I don't want her to get sick and miss my birthday. She did that to me one time.

Debbie: If I get married, I wear my peach dress. Maybe my flowered dress.

Josh: Yeah, yeah, that one. I like it. I do.

Debbie: Maybe my peach dress. The one with the belt. My hair, I would . . .

Josh: Make it curly.

Debbie: (purses her lips) Josh. No. I would get a haircut. My mom says so you can see my face. I would put it up in a bow. I would have some flowers. I would walk down with my mom and my dad.

Josh: And I would walk down with my mom and dad. I think we would all meet in front. In a church.

Debbie: Outside.

Josh: Okay, outside. I would wear a suit. Like my wedding suit. My mom would go pick it up. You know, a tuxedo. With a little tie, you know, with black and yellow dots. I like that.

For the talking part, I would say that we love, and we marry and . . .

Debbie: Josh, can I talk?

Josh: Sorry. Go ahead.

Debbie: I would say I love him. And I give my life for him. . . .

Josh: (giggles) Oooo, she want me now!

Debbie: And I would say I want to go out with him. And I would say I love him and I want to be with him and I want him as my boyfriend. If Joe McIntyre shows up I would tell him too bad, I am marry now.

Josh: I would say in church I love Debbie very lot and she has a cute little face.

Debbie: (giggles)

Josh: (pats her cheek) And because we love now and she is my wife and we have wedding and stuff and we say I do because we love now. Someone get divorce, then we not see them again.

Debbie: What? That's not true!

Josh: Yes, it is because when Grannie and him not see each other. We don't do that. I love her a lot (reaches for her).

Debbie: Don't touch me.

Josh: And because we love . . .

Debbie: *In* love you say it.

Josh: (sighs) I mean because we *in* love, and marry, I be working and she be working, too. We get our paychecks and we go to the bank and pick up our money and save some money in the bank. That is very important.

Me and my mom went to get a promise ring at Wal-Mart where I was workin' then. Cause I working at there, now I don't no more. My mom take me with her to get a promise ring for Debbie because she is my heart and because I want to, so I did it.

I know what I wanted. We look around and the girl, the lady show us some with cerbic zirconius but I like one with a heart. The heart one had a little diamond and that's what I want. I tell the lady the diamond is better for Debbie. It hadda be real.

Debbie want a ring so bad and the heart promise was good. It was beautiful one and when I give it to her, I say "Debbie, will you marry me?" and she say "Okay, sure." (Debbie extends her left hand, wiggling her ring finger).

I think we might have one baby.

Debbie: PU-lease! Shut up, Josh? How do your mom feel about this?

Josh: (slowly) I think my mom wouldn't like it and if Debbie had a baby, I would go over to her house and tell her, "Debbie, it be okay. I be your husband." Once when Debbie was in the hospital and Jean took me to see her and I took Debbie's hand right here and I tell her "Debbie, don't worry. It's okay. It's me." She would be pushing from the baby and I would hold her hand so tight and she would push and then I say "There is our baby" and Debbie would say "Yeah." I think it's a girl. I think so.

Debbie: I would think I have a boy.

Josh: (sternly) Debbie. You had a girl.

After you have a baby, you gotta be careful to her and Debbie will be away workin' and I stay at home with the baby. I would be clean up the baby, change diapers. I would get money, my money from the bank to buy diapers and stuff. Babies cost a lot of money.

If Debbie don't want a baby and I do then we got a problem.

Debbie: On *Roseanne*, member what happen? Roseanne had to go for tests to see if she have a baby. And she was pregnant.

Josh: (solemnly) Yes, she was. Anyway, on *Roseanne* . . .

Debbie: (whispers) I love you, Josh.

Josh: Debbie. Please. Not now. I'm talking. Anyway, Roseanne's sister, her husband, got kill on his motorcycle. And Roseanne cry so hard, but her husband in the hospital and she go see him and he have tears in his eyes and she tell him "I love you" like that. Then he was okay.

Debbie: If Josh get hurt in accident or somethin' like that, I would call 911. And I would say "Can somebody come because my boyfriend is in accident. . . ."

Josh: (whispers behind his hand) Debbie, say "husband."

Debbie: Sorry. I mean "my husband." I would tell 'em my address is North West 13th Place, Gainesville, Florida and my zip code is . . . What's my zip code, Mom? Anyway, my area code is 32605.

Josh: What's the house number? You gotta give them the house number. Debbie, the number for your house.

Debbie: I don't know. Anyway, while we wait, I would sit with him . . .

Josh: And hold my hand.

Debbie: Yeah, yeah. I would hold his hand and sit with him and talk to him and make him comfaful. I would say "Baby, you're gonna be okay. They're on the way." Just like TV.

I'm going to move out someday from my mom's and when Josh moves out from his mom and dad, he's gonna take me with him. And so we have to get marry, I guess, I don't know.

Josh: We get marry so we can live in a house.

Debbie: (holds up a finger) With a pool.

Josh: Yeah, with a pool.

Just me and Debbie so we clean our house. We ask my mom and dad and Debbie's mom, Jean, over to visit. We make tacos and have fun. But they don't live in our house, they just visit. Okay, Debbie?

Debbie: PU-lease!

Update: Josh has since asked Debbie to marry him and she has agreed. He's been shopping for an engagement ring. Her heart condition has become worse.

Ellen Gajewski and Christopher Walken

Indianapolis, Indiana/ New York, New York

*E*ighteen-year-old Ellen Gajewski smiles shyly. She brushes the grass as she sits demurely on the newly mown lawn outside Gray Brother's Cafeteria in Mooresville, Indiana. Born in Indianapolis, Ellen will graduate from high school in 1996 and works part-time at Remax Realty, labelling postcards. She's had boyfriends, she says, but they're really boys who are friends. The love of her life, she says, the man she's going to marry (though it will be news to him), is movie star Christopher Walken. Her Remax paychecks go into the bank because she's "saving up to go to New York so we can get married," she says seriously.

I love him (shrugs). After I graduate, then I am going to New York. I get money at my job at Remax. I do postcards. I got three checks. I got $38. I'm saving it to go to New York. Christopher Walken wants me to go there. I write him a letter. In New York. I don't like James Bond, though. He is too old for me. Way too old. He had grey hair. He is not too old for my mother. But she likes Robert, that's my dad.

I went to the prom with Drew. He's wonderful. He is short. He's graduate. He had a job, but he got fired. I wore a dress to the prom. A prom dress. He wore grey pants. He only had one flower. Here (pats her chest) and I had flowers on my wrist so I can do this (waves her arm gracefully and extends her hand). His flower was white. Drew had a father and he took us. They had music and food. We dance. I like dancing. I dance with Allan. He's my friend's boyfriend. She dance with Drew. We traded.

I have another friend. A guy. His name is Greg. He is 20, I think, or 26. Greg likes Christopher Walken, too, so we talk about him. He wants to marry me, Christopher Walken does. I want to go to see him in New York. I love him. I would wear a dress. A white dress. I would have flowers and music. I like him in the movies.

Greg rode his bike to see me in the hospital. I had heart surgery. Now it is just a line on my chest. It's okay now. He rode his bike over to see me. It was a long way, but he want to see me. I have a scar. I have to have surgery. I told Dr. King before I went to sleep, I say, "Please be careful with my heart" and he say, "Okay, I will." Always used to fall asleep, now I don't do that. I am better now. Greg is a nice guy. He come to the hospital to see me. We not say anything, we just talking. He bring me flowers. Greg and I are friends. We just talking. We talk about Christopher Walken and movies.

I like Drew and Greg. I like both. Cause Greg is my friend. Drew is more my boyfriend. I like Drew. I kiss him a little bit. I kiss Christopher Walken, too, a little bit. It was pretty cool.

With Drew, I go to movies. To his house. We have pizza together. Kissing at his house. It's so cute, romantic.

My friends are Sarah and Jenny. Sarah is 17 and Jenny is 10. Robin is my friend, too. Sarah and Jenny come to my birthday party. We talk about boys. Sarah has a boyfriend, his name is Brian. Boys like girls. I like Christopher Walken. He's very cute. Boys are nice. If one was not nice to me, I would be very upset. Christopher Walken is very nice and he would go out with me. He will kiss me on the lips. We could go places. But he and James Bond would fight over me (giggles).

My brother is 23. His name is Tony. He has a girlfriend, Libby. She is very kind and 22 and she is gorgeous. She is at school and they will get married. Tony has only Libby forever.

When I go to New York, I wash my hair. Christopher and I go for a walk a little bit. We have ice cream and coffee. I like vanilla. I wear a white wedding dress. A white one. I have a band and a thing that covers your face. Christopher Walken will lift up the thing and kiss me on the lips. Womens wear wedding dress, not men. Mens wear suit. Not me, I wear a dress. I will throw the flowers to my mom.

I will not have any babies. They cry. Sarah is too old to have a baby. Not Libby either. Not Mom either. She has two, me and Tony. That's enough. She have two, so she don't want me to have a baby. My mom tells me about babies. I know that stuff.

A kiss is very cool. It is nice and kind. Make me feel wonderful. If it's Christopher Walken. When I kiss Drew, I don't think about Christopher Walken. I can't do that. But Christopher is the best guy. I have *Batman Returns*, he's in that movie. And I have *Scanners*. I have his pictures. I kiss him very much. I will go to New York. Christopher Walken is my type, that means who I love. He is so gorgeous (rolls her eyes, giggles).

For my boyfriend, I have Drew. Greg is my friend. I kiss him, but as a friend. He's not my type, but he is my friend. Drew is my type. Greg is my friend, friend, friend, but not my boyfriend. Drew makes me feel like a girlfriend. I kiss him a lot. He likes that. He has a job. I don't know where he works at. I go to his graduation one time. I just go up and say, "Hey, Drew, how's it goin'?" He is white. He has blonde hair. Greg has yellow hair. Different. Drew is 18. He is more my type.

But Christopher Walken is the one I will marry. He is waiting for me to go to New York, making movies and stuff. He is the best. He is 49, but that is not old. He is just so cool.

TO HONOR AND CHERISH

My family didn't think we should get married. They figured I could do better, but I didn't think so. There were people who said I was slower and shouldn't get married and that didn't make me feel so good.
> —Don Thibault

Come to think of it, nobody could believe me that I was gonna get married. They didn't think I was abable of it or some-thing.

My mom just said, "Oh" and my dad said if I didn't have more than 75 people, he'd pay for it. We had 74.
> —Edith Peterson

Allen and Nadine Babcock

Ellensburg, Washington

S he follows close behind him, shoulders stooped, peering over the rims of her glasses, carrying an amazingly massive purse. She smiles nervously as he pulls out a chair for her at Frazzini's, their favorite pizza place. Allen, 41, lived in an institution in Oregon for ten years and his wife Nadine, 34, was admitted to one when she was nine. The couple met in 1977 and were married in 1991. Her brother in Denver, the only family member she'd seen in 24 years, accepted the invitation to give away the bride. As Allen begins their story, Nadine pulls crayons and paper from her purse and begins to color.

Allen: (speaks loudly over restaurant noise) We are newlyweds. The weddin' was okay. Everybody said they really enjoy it. My brother came.

I met Nadine back in '77 cause I move here. I like the town so much so I want to move here. My mom and dad and brother move quite a bit when I was little. In 1960, I was in institution for ten years in Oregon. A girl I know induced me to Nadine. I thought she was really nice. Couple year before we get married, we know each other. I will be 41 in 13 days.

___

Nadine: (Shyly looks at her husband, then at the tabletop) I think he cute when I see him. I don wanna tell nobody how old I am. I was a baby when my family just drop me off at intitution.

___

Allen: Before we got married, we was livin' together for almost two years. I did wanna get married, but I want to make sure. Her sister and her mom say it was good idea. Since I got in contact with her family, she didn't see them since she was about two years old. I like Nadine cause we could talk and I like that and doin' things together.

___

Nadine: (somberly) Long time ago I had a little baby. The doctor say no. People say she couldn't care for him, so she give baby up for doption. That was way back in '74. I name baby Heather. I was in hospital and they don't let me see her. They push me in the hallway and I got hurt in my side. After doctor took the baby outta my stomach, they did operation. I couldn't sit up. It didn't work and they hadda do it again.

___

Allen: We talk about our own baby, but we don't have enough money. One thing we don't need is someone to spend more money! We need to talk to doctor and see if we would be possible to do operation so Nadine could have a baby. I like to have a house first for baby, too. It's big responsibility. We go bowling and sometimes we go to a movie, but we don't have too much money for that.

Nadine: (smiles) My dress was all white and had a belt on it. I had white flowers. My bridesmaid was my friend. My brother give me away. Jim. I didn't see him for long time.

Allen: I had a guy for my bestman. He name was Jim, too. It was at two o'clock. Her brother took us out for dinner. Nadine want hamburger and french fries, but her brother wouldn't let her have that, so she had ribs like I did. Her brother came from Denver, Colorado. He give us $50 for wedding present. That was very nice of him.

Nadine: (stops coloring) Sometime I yell at Allen.

Allen: I do all the cooking. I was at work one day and she burned her fingers on the burner. It was very bad. So she go to the hospital. I work with a couple people. It's a good job. It's called attendant support and I meet a lot of people. A guy I work with, he needs me to help him because he's on a wheelchair.

Nadine: (selects a new pencil, hunches over the table) I do cleaning. At bakery.

Allen: We live down in the basement and there are five apartments.

Nadine: (looks up) There are lots of spiders. I find one in sink. I kill it with hot water (grins proudly).

Allen: We are getting a house. We hadda go see if we qualify and we did qualify and so we fill out qualify forms. Then when a okay comes, they can start on our house. Maybe next year.

Nadine: I want a cat. We can't have no cats now. Landlord says no cats. I want a bird. A bird and a cat.

Allen: I would like to have our own place. When something breaks now, it is hard to get hold of our landlord. He is pretty hard to get hold of when we are complaining. I would like to have a house with more than one bedroom. Then Nadine could have her cats.

People got to make sure they get along good, quite good before they get married. They should not rush into getting married and they get a divorce. One thing about Nadine that bugs me is she carry so much stuff with her in her bag all the time. It's so heavy!

Nadine: (hauls her bag from the floor, drops it heavily on the table) Anybody make fun of us or be mean, I hit 'em with my bag. He bug me when he play pool too much. But he cute.

Allen: I like lots of things about Nadine. She stick up for me when nobody else does. She say somethin' if people make fun of me. That not happen too much. Most people know me. We play cribbage, me and Nadine. Last time we play cribbage, she beat me. But she cheat when I go to the bathroom. She change my peg with her peg (laughs). We can do things together when we're married. I cook hamburgers quite good. We don't hold hands very much like some people. Sometimes if I go somewhere, she want to go with me and if she go somewhere, she want me to go with her.

Nadine: I like bein' married cause he cooks for me. I like him better. I wash dishes and he cooks. Meat too spensive. We buy chicken. It cheaper. He bake it.

Allen: We got married at Catholic Church and before we get married we hadda go so they could see how happy we were. They ask us questions about lots of things. They do that to everybody, not just me and Nadine. This man was priest; I don't know if there is any woman priest, but there might be.

Nadine: All the people used to get together and put water on your head and you was babtize. I get him babtize (she nods toward Allen). They drop water on his head.

Allen: When I got babtize, they put Nadine's name and my friend's name down as my godparents.

Nadine: Someone beat me up a long time ago. It was nother guy. For some reason, he beat me up. I cry. That don't happen no more with Allen.

Allen: We got a VCR so we watch movies sometimes. I was pretty nervous. The night before the wedding, I was so nervous I could hardly see. I sleep on the couch.

Nadine: That not very good! My husband sleep on the couch! Sometime I get mad at him. Sometime I get upset, too. I don't like to see the news. On TV, people get shot and dying. I don't like that.

Allen: Mostly when she get upset when she think about her daughter and when people say "no" and when people move away. Staff go away a lot. I like 'em and then they go away, leave. I don't like that. We don't have any very good friends, but we know people we see every day. Like staff. Some people we work with. We don't like when people leave us.

Her nickname is Jitterbug cause when she was little girl, if they put the music on, she would start dancing. Nadine likes to color and she always make bookmarks with pretty colors like church windows like she doin' now. She make 'em for everybody and she never give me one until I bug her and then she give me a nice one, too.

When Nadine was a little girl, she love her sandbox and she didn't like nobody messin' around with her sandbox. One day a man came to put her sandbox on his truck and take it away. Nadine get so mad, she bit the tire! (Laughs. Nadine smiles and colors vigorously). That's what I like about Nadine. I like to be married to her so she can proteck me! If she don't bite 'em, she hit 'em with her big heavy purse!

Update: Nadine died of a brain aneurysm on December 21, 1992. She was 35. "She collapsed at home one evening," says Allen, who continues to live in Ellensburg, Washington. "I call the ambulance and she was taken to our local hospital. Then she went to a bigger hospital in Yakima. Then she was air-lifted to a hospital in Seattle where she had two surgeries. She lived another ten days in intensive care. I stay with her the whole time." Allen made the decision to disconnect Nadine's life support after speaking with her doctors. "She die peacefully about four hours later," he says.

Barry and Wendy Smith

Toronto, Ontario

"*I*t's important to have a sense of humor if you're married to Barry," Wendy, 42, says dryly. She shares a high rise apartment in a seniors complex with the object of her barb, her husband of six years. As an active and vocal member of the self-advocacy organization People First, Barry, 45, has appeared in many public awareness campaigns. He is proudest of a full color poster, featuring him in his usher's tuxedo at his workplace, the Roy Thompson Concert Hall in downtown Toronto. Sometimes he wears his tuxedo home from work on the subway "so people will know I have a good job."

Barry, who was born in 1948, lived in an institution in Orillia, Ontario. He later moved to Barrie's Adult Occupational Centre, where he met Wendy. She left the institution first; he followed later to Toronto, where they were married in 1987. Barry had occasional difficulty getting along with Wendy's mother, but got some advice from television. "You know that one show of *The Flintstones* where Fred keeps saying over and over, 'I love my mother-in-law. I love my mother-in-law.' Well, be darned if it didn't work. That's one thing the Flintstones taught me that actually works."

The couple scoffs at the idea of having children; they like their role as aunt and uncle of various nieces and nephews because "we can have fun with them and then give them back!" Wendy, born in 1951, was sterilized in the institution when she was 15 "so that was that," she says. They have a cat, Scamper, who "thinks your feet are hockey pucks when you walk by." The couple argues and bickers in what is obviously a long-standing and usually affable form of communication.

Wendy: (inspecting her nails) I had went out with a guy before, but he wasn't very good so I ditched him. As I got to know Barry, I changed my mind around about him. We knew each other in the school for about two years and then we lived together for two years and then we started deciding whether we were going to get married or not. My dad didn't like us living together because he thought we should be older and I told him I was getting older by the minute.

Barry: I don't think it was anything that made me attracted to Wendy. I mean anything special. I just more or less wanted a companion. In the institution there was only so much you could do and only so many places you could go. Like they had dances, but either you dance with a girl or if they didn't want to, you danced with a boy. When we got out, living together was unheard of. I think I was one of the first people to do it. My parents weren't for it at all. My father said no way, but I said this is what I want and that's that, so I sorta talked them into it. My father divorced my mother. My dad didn't show up for my wedding because my mother was there and they can't stand being in the same room. I don't remember what year that was. . . .

Wendy: (stares at her husband) You're telling me you don't remember the year of our wedding? It was 1987, dear.

Barry: It was just a small wedding at a church in Sudbury. It was one of these churches on the university campus. Her uncle was an architect and he designs all kinds of buildings and they have a committee that goes around and just the day before we got married, Wendy's uncle got an award for designing the same church we got married in.

I was working and I don't think Wendy was working when we got married. I worked for a place called Motorola and they fixed televisions. I worked in the kitchen. It was hard at first because we didn't have much money. By the time we bought food, there wasn't much left.

Wendy: Sometimes we had to phone his dad when we had no money for food. It took some getting used to some of his bad habits. It took a long time to get used to his personality and his demands. His pants have to be just so. He can't even iron a shirt or a pair of pants.

Barry: (runs a hand over his hair) Oh, I can, but it takes me an hour or more to do it! We just do chores. She does some things and I do some things, unless I have to go to work. She's right, I'm hopeless at ironing and I do it a totally different way than she or anyone else does it. I even burnt my shirt once.

Wendy: And it was a Roy Thompson Hall shirt he wears at work. I had to try to get the stain out and it finally came out.

Barry: I was talking to another boy awhile ago and he said all you had to do was walk down Yonge Street and girls would come up to you and ask you if you wanted to go to bed. I told him that never happen to me and besides I don't think that story is true. I've walked down Yonge Street plenty of times and nobody's ever come up to me with that type of thing. Unless you actually know a hooker or something or if you're looking for something, well, that's different. And if that ever happen, I would tell them I'd have to go with them for a year before that type of thing because you never know if you're right for each other, if you're going to get along. I think I'd want to go out for three or four years or maybe more until we were comfortable. Then you can talk about that other type of thing. I think Wendy and I knew each other pretty close to five years before, you know.

Wendy: I don't think we've really figured out yet what the best thing is about being married. If parents didn't want their kids to get married or live together, they should let the kids decide on their own. They have minds of their own and they can decide.

Barry: It's not personal against their kids, but parents think their kids will fail outside the institution. One of the philosophy things I came up with was let the person fall down. Let them pick themselves up and go again. They will learn. Parents are afraid if they have a baby, it will come out retarded. Some parents think their kids will just die out here in the community because they don't know how to go shopping or pay their rent. They don't know nothing about sex and they can't describe it to you. If they can't describe it, parents are

afraid they can't look after a baby and that's why people get sterilized so they can't have a baby ever.

They wanted to bring my sister out of the institution to live in a
group home with boys and girls and my parents thought in their
mind "What if one of the boys approach her and says do you want
to have sex?" and she says yes, but she don't know what it means or
anything. What happens if she gets pregnant and has a baby? Whose
fault is that? The parents? Or society? Who takes the blame?
Nobody know to answer to that one. Who makes sure it doesn't happen in the first place?

Wendy: (gazes through the sliding glass doors to the tiny balcony)
We can never have children because, well, I had an operation. I
knew what it was for. My mom came up to the institution for it. I
was only 15. Now, I wouldn't want to bring a kid into the world
anyways. We're on family benefits* and it's really rough. Kids are
expensive so we couldn't do it even if we wanted to. We babysit for
a friend when they go to a show or out to supper. One time she
stayed overnight. I like it this way. For people like us who really
want kids but can't have them, it gives a chance to know what it
feels like to have kids. They should make teenagers who are having
sex but think they won't get a baby to rent a kid for a weekend and
then at the end you could ask them if they would really want to have
a baby. Then maybe they'd be more careful with their birth control
or whatever because they'd know. They should make them talk to
people with AIDS so they'd know it could happen to them. Maybe
that would open their eyes.

------

* *Social assistance.*

Barry: I was a little older than Wendy when I got the operation.
They did it in the institution all the time because they didn't want
babies in there. They used the Pill, too, but for the ones who
wouldn't take it or threw it away, then they operated.

Wendy and I argue and fight. Someone told me a few years ago
that if you don't argue, you're not living. If you argue and fight, at
least you're normal.

Wendy: (guffaws) Are you sure you're normal? I'm not so sure,
dear!

My name used to be Morris before I married him (jerks her
thumb toward Barry). I changed my name to his because he was always teasing me and calling me Morris the Cat, Morris the Cat.
Now he can't do that so he keeps quiet.

The worst thing about marriage is having a man tell you what to
do. And what to wear. Like I had runs in my nylons and he said
"That isn't any good. Go change them." I didn't like being told what
to do in the institution either. If something happened to Barry, I
don't think I'd start out again looking for a man. I could live on my
own and sometimes I think it would be better. It's my birthday soon
and he got me a camera and I was hoping for a big fat diamond ring!

Barry: At my job, I get to see some of the shows. I got to see Ella
Fitzgerald when she was there. What I do is wear my tuxedo and
hand out programs and then I show you what section to go in and
what door to go through and I tell people where the bathrooms are.
All the arms on the seats have numbers on them, but sometimes
people get confused and you have to help them. We're trained in
everything from fire safety to bomb threats. We nearly had a bomb
threat once; they put on extra police. We've had the Queen and all
her men. We've had many special people like Roger Whitaker, and I

can't remember them all. Sometimes thousands of people come to watch just one old guy play the piano. Sometimes it's a little boring. Roger Whitaker was there twice and Wendy got his autograph.

Wendy: I like to keep in touch with people on the phone. Going out is so expensive. I had a job doing packaging, but the company close down. I'd like to work at Roy Thompson Hall, too, but he keeps harping that you have to know how to read and write and spell.

Barry: When we got married, I think I wore a suit jacket and a white shirt and a pair of pants. As a matter of fact, when I got off the bus, I pick up the wrong suitcase because it looked just like mine. Boy, was I embarrassed when I opened it up. There were all these, you know, ladies' things like bras and underwear. We called the bus and they found the lady with my suitcase with all my wedding stuff in it. Another thing I learned was when you go to the bathroom at a hotel for your wedding, don't lock the bathroom door. I did and couldn't get out so I had to stand in the bathtub and they got a guy like a football player to crash through the door. I was shaking people's hands and they were saying, "Congratulations and, oh, I heard you were locked in the bathroom." We went to Niagara Falls for our honeymoon. It's just lovely there. Lots of people have ended up dead there because it's so dangerous.

Wendy: It's hard to say what I like about Barry. He's pretty good for a beginner. It's important to have a sense of humor when you're married to Barry. Sometimes his personality will flare up, especially when he has a headache. But other times he's an angel. When he's an angel, he does the housework. He brings me things like books. He's broughten me tickets to a show at Roy Thompson Hall but they're mostly for old fashioned shows he likes. He's 43 and I haven't hit the big Four-O yet.

_____

Barry: In the institution, there was staff around 24 hours a day. If I wanted to go to Wendy's room, I had to hide in the closet when staff would come in. We did break the rules and then we'd be in punishment. One guy got caught with another boy and they made him scrub the washroom day in and day out. Finally he couldn't take it any more and he ran away. He was only wearing a shirt and pants and it was in the middle of December and he got as far as the railroad tracks and he froze and they tried to unfroze him but they couldn't, so he just died frozen. That was the only way he could get out. We didn't believe it, so they took a bunch of us to a room where when you're dead they wrap you up like a mummy and they took us to see him. I was about nine or ten then and I think they told us that to scare us so we'd all behave. I got very sick from it because I'd never seen that before.

I remember seeing the girls and we had socials and dances, but we knew the rule was "Don't touch." I had one friend once in there who was a girl. I came back from working one day and found out she had been sent to another institution because we got to be good friends. I didn't even say goodbye or good luck to her. They didn't like relationships. They didn't want to think about babies or anything because that would be too difficult to deal with. They don't want to deal with boyfriend and girlfriend stuff or sex education. They brought in one man from a university once to talk about sex, but he just talked to us once in a group of guys. I know one girl who got pregnant and they took her away and then she wasn't pregnant anymore.

Wendy: (folds her arms) People in the institution treated us like babies. They even called us "kids" or "trainees." If you were watching a movie on movie night, and you were sitting with a guy and you kissed or something, the staff would separate you or send one of you to your room. Just like little kids who weren't behaving the way staff wanted them to.

Barry: It's hard to say what I like best about Wendy. Sometimes if I have a problem with Wendy, I ask one of the girl ushers at work. They can see it and explain it from a woman's point without getting all mad and yelling at me. They give me suggestions about what to try and that helps. Sometimes it's easier to talk to someone else who's a woman.

We like to watch movies and we do it a lot. Marriage is not like the movies, that's for sure. If you think it'll be all romantic all the time, you can forget that!

Relationships can be good, especially if someone is lonely. They should have someone. If you fall, you pick yourselves and each other up and go on. And family benefits aren't as much if you're a couple so it almost forces people to stay lonely and alone just so they can have a few more dollars for groceries. You can be in an institution with hundreds of people and you can still be the loneliest person on earth.

Wendy: (shrugs) I don't think I'd ever get married again. It takes too long to train a husband, so maybe I'll just be happy with this one. Okay, dear?

Update: Barry and Wendy separated in November 1993. "Wendy and I will not be getting back together," says Barry, who moved into his own apartment in Etobicoke, a Toronto suburb. After many months of "yelling and screaming and complaining most of the time, I just couldn't take it anymore," he says simply. "Now I am looking for a new girlfriend that might want to marry me and live with me and not yell and complain. If you got any suggestions, please let me know as I don't even know how to go about looking for one."

Phil and
Wendy Allen

Burnaby, British Columbia

*T*he 28-year age difference doesn't seem to matter much
to Phil and Wendy Allen, 64 and 36. Wendy stocks shelves at a
Fabricland store in Surrey, making her way to work by bus; he
spends his days as a dedicated speaker for people with disabilities. He's a member of many community boards, and
talks to social workers, school children, and human service
workers about equality, dignity, and respect. Both are guests
on a weekly FM radio program, broadcast in the Vancouver
area; they discuss issues and concerns to people with disabilities.

Phil, who was born in Saskatoon, Saskatchewan in 1927,
went to live at the Training School in Moose Jaw when he was
a teenager. He finally walked out at 27, climbed aboard a
train, and headed west, "as far away from the place as I
could get." In their small apartment, he worries about being
put in a nursing home as he gets older. Wendy arrives out of
breath and dishevelled from running home and explains the
transit workers went on strike that afternoon. Hearing her
husband's words, she soothes, "No way, Babe. No way will
you have to go back to an institution. I'm here. I'll take care

of you. You just forget that now," she bubbles, then adds happily, "Aren't you looking forward to going out for supper? I
am! I've been thinking about it all day!"

Later, at a restaurant within walking distance of their apartment, she practices her reading skills on the menu. She's
been taking classes at the local community college. She carefully reads items on the menu to Phil, whose dimming eyesight
makes it difficult for him to decide. "I know you like liver and
onions, Babe, but listen to this: 'Homestyle ribs, mar. .in. .nated
in a . . . special. . sauce that will . . bring . . you . . back . . for
more.' I'd like to come back for more. I think I'll have that."

Phil: (wanders slowly through the small apartment, showing knick-
knacks) Most people don't have anybody to talk to. That's terrible.
People shouldn't be treated that way, put away from their family in
institutions. I want to stay right here. I'm 64 and I don't want to go
to no home somewhere. Here is my home. I was born in Saskatoon.
I have no idea if I got brothers and sisters. Never even talked to
them. People told me I couldn't be "productive" so I was in the institution in Moose Jaw. When I took off from there, I got a lot of different jobs in Vancouver. I washed cars. I parked cars. It was hard. I
went to places and they look at me and say they couldn't hire me
cause I'd be bad for business.

I had a girlfriend in the institution, but staff never knew about it. You had to be sneaky. If you got caught, they put you in the side room.* As far as I'm concerned, it was a bad thing. People on the outside will never know the truth about those places, what went on in there. I never thought I'd get married. I sort of figured I could just wish.

I met Wendy at a nice little party and it was love at first sight. We lived together. We married seven or eight years ago. Went out for only six months. Her family like me right away quick. It was such a long time ago, I forget how I ask her to marry me. We went to two classes before we got married. The priest was real nice and never said boo to us about bein' handicapped.

We had a three-layer cake. I don't like the fake ones. It was a real cake and we ate it. Friends of mine got married and their fake cake sits in their house and is all dusty. What good is that? Might as well eat it.

I never wanted to have kids and Wendy can't have kids anyways. We got lots of relations, so we got lots of kids around anyways. When we're done with 'em, we can give 'em back!

Wendy looked just beautiful on our wedding day. I looked pretty good, too. Yep, that was a nice day. It was a little cloudy in the morning and cleared up in the afternoon. We had the reception in the afternoon.

Wendy: (rushes in, breathless, shrugs off her coat and kicks her shoes down the hall) I'm so sorry I'm late! I had to run all the way. I thought "Oh, no! Don't go on strike today!" But they did anyways,

---

* *Isolation room used for punishment.*

so now I can hardly breathe! I'll just be a minute. Hello, Babe, how was your day? (She disappears into the bedroom to change.)

Phil: Wendy collects spoons. She don't collect as much pins and buttons as I do, but then I been doin' it for years. I got 'em from everywhere.

Wendy: (calls out from the bedroom) I like to have liver and onions when we go out to eat. I never used to, I used to think it tasted like a rubber shoe! My mother would always say, "Why do you think it tastes like a rubber shoe?" and I would say, "Because it tastes like a rubber shoe." We don't go out to eat very much because it's expensive (enters the living room) and we can't afford it, so I been lookin' forward to this all day. Haven't you, Babe? You look very nice tonight.

Phil: I got such soft hair. When I wash it, I can't do anything with it. See?

Wendy: That's true. That's true about his hair. Here, let me fix it. There, ready to go? It'll be a nice walk. Come on, I'll help you . . .

Wendy: (sliding into a green vinyl booth at the restaurant) We met at a friend's party and it was, what do you call it, love at first sight. We started going out and seeing each other and what not. I thought he was so nice. A cool guy. We went together for a year. I used to live in North Burnaby and the buses were just crazy, so I told him I'd move in with him and I did for six months. I told my mom and she was okay with it. But when he told his stepmother, she thought nah, nah, nah! She was old fashioned and in her time, you didn't do that. She got used to us, and was real happy when we said we were gettin' married. A lot of handicapped people can't even get married. They're not allowed to. It was pretty easy for us. My older sister, Janet, likes Phil a lot. My younger sister, well, she likes Phil okay. She's married to, get this, a magician. How's that, I got a magician for a brother-in-law! So if my sister can be married to a magician, I figure being married to a guy that's handicapped is probably a lot easier! Right, Babe?

Phil: (shakes his head) Not letting people get married if they want to be together is very cruel. Why would people ever do that? We all need to have somebody and to make somebody be alone for their life, I don't understand it. Whether you're handicapped or not doesn't mean you can't love somebody or you can't clean up the house. A lot of people have someone to come in and help them with their money or give them a hand with shopping or their laundry. But if two people can live together and be married, they can help each other, too.

Wendy: It's just like a person with a mental handicap having a child. I've got a couple of friends that are handicapped. My best girlfriend has a little girl and another friend that's handicapped just had a baby. So I've got two friends. People say about them they've got no business having children because they're handicapped, even though they're good mothers. But the thing is we have the same right to bear children as anybody else. It's got to be our decision and we need people to help us make the decision. . ..

Phil: Something else . . .

Wendy: (puts a hand on his arm) Excuse me, Babe, let me finish.
I've learned this at school not to interrupt when someone is talking,
so let me finish and then you can have your turn, okay?

It's the same with anybody. Some people will make good
parents and some people aren't so good. Being handicapped doesn't
automatic mean you're terrible. People think if you're handicapped,
you'll automatic have a handicapped baby and that's not true. It's
just wrong to say that nobody who is handicapped should have a
baby.

(Takes a deep breath) I can't have a child. I've had a hysterec-
tomy so I can never have children. Phil understands that. I had a
child, a daughter when I was 19 and I was still living at home.
Sometimes I don't like to talk about it because it still upsets me, but
I'm okay so I'll talk about it. I've told Phil this story. My mother
was very, very, very angry. She came into my room and my father
came in and had to pull her off. She really freaked out and told me I
wasn't married and shouldn't be doing things like this. I wanted to
tell her there were lots of single mothers out there and I wasn't the
first. She gave me the alternative that if I was going to keep the
baby, I could move out. I was only 19 and I didn't know enough. I
wasn't ready to move out of the house. So I gave her up. It was so
hard. I would have given anything to keep her and I still think about
her. It wasn't my decision, but if I had kept her, I would have had to
leave home. I didn't have a job. I would have had no way of paying
my rent or buying groceries. If I had a job, who would have looked
after my daughter? So that was it. And I got my tubes tied and now I
can never have children. I didn't want my tubes tied either because I
thought if I ever met the right man and got married, maybe we'd
like to have a child. But Phil understands. We have each other and I
think that's the main thing. (smiles) I have a budgie. He's my baby;
his name is Dennis.

Phil: We've got some friends who fight all the time. They call each other names and I don't know what they're going to do. I think it's because people don't take enough time to really find someone to marry. They get married cause they think it's a good idea because their friends are doing it.

Wendy: (beams at him) There are so many things I like about Phil. He's a really nice guy. He's got a good sense of humor and he makes me laugh a lot. He always has a good sense of humor.

Phil: People should be happy. Sad's not going to get you nowhere. Life's too short to be sad and miserable. I've been around a long time and I've seen a lot of people mad and sad and their kids don't turn out too good. You have to make yourself happy in this world. You have to pay attention to the kids and listen to them and talk to them. They don't teach kids enough about sex and the body and what it's for. They should start with little kids and tell them right things because they hear about it anyways. They figure people with handicaps don't think about that stuff, but we do just like everyone else. That's why they used to separate the kids in the institution. That's the way it was, but we're supposed to be smarter now. The law is going to change. When people are living in group homes, they're going to be able to have their boyfriends or girlfriends over and be allowed to have sex or whatever in their own homes. Everybody has those feelings so staff and parents just better get used to it.

Wendy: My father wanted boys. He had four girls instead. He wanted sons, but we all turned out to be girls. I told him once, "You can't put us back. You gotta take us even though we turned out to be girls." I wanted to do things with my dad like boys got to do. Oh, sure, he'd take me to hockey games, but I wanted to go fishing so I told him even though I was a girl, I could still put worms on the hook anyways. He'd go fishing with his friend and maybe the friend didn't want a little girl along. My last name used to be Kaufman. The kids in school used to tease me and called me Cough Syrup.

Phil: I think we went to a show on our first date. It's too expensive now. It's $7.50. That's just terrible. We haven't been to a show in about three years. You end up paying $25 once you buy some popcorn and pop, so we just can't do it. Sometimes we just rent a movie and watch it at home, but that's still expensive. We don't have much money, so we have to be very, very careful.

I enjoy Wendy's company a lot. We like to do the same things. We like to walk around in the malls. We like being together.

Wendy: (nods) We hold hands a lot. Phil is a very affectionate man. Whenever we go for a walk, we hold hands. Some of our friends never do and we think that's sad.

My sister's two girls came over to our place. We took the girls to the mall and then for lunch. We took them to that place, what's it called, Babe? He can say it better. It's Chunky Cheeses. That's it. The girls loved it.

Phil: Like I was saying before, I don't want to ever have to go into a nursing home when I get old. It'll be too much like the institution in Saskatchewan and I just couldn't stand it. I just want to live in my own home until I pass away. They're changin' the laws in that way, too. I'm pretty healthy and so it should be my choice where I finish out my life.

Wendy: (Busily rearranges the cutlery) Don't worry, Babe. That'll never happen as long as I'm around to take care of you. That's part of the deal when you are married, you know. You look after each other when one gets old and Phil is quite a bit older than me by about 28 years. But you shouldn't be selfish when you're married, so I promised Phil I would take care of him if he gets old or sick. He understands that, but sometimes he gets a little nervous, you know, that someone would try to take him away from me and put him in a home for old people. I tell him "Honey, don't worry."

PARENT-HOOD

Love doesn't sit there like a stone, it has to be made, like bread; remade all the time, made new.
—Ursula K. Le Guin

A family is a unit composed not only of children, men, women, but an occasional animal and the common cold.
—Ogden Nash

Lamarr and Kim Johnson, sons Trevor, Kevin

Culver City, California

*T*he television blares with afternoon soaps as Kim, 37, feeds baby Trevor, bouncing him with the time-tested bounce mothers discover for getting their youngsters to sleep. Kevin, a three and a half-year-old powerhouse of energy, tests his parents' patience as he darts around the toy-strewn apartment. LaMarr, 31, a handsome and softspoken L.A. Lakers fan, quietly but firmly reins in his son, apologizing over one shoulder, "Kevin really needs to take a nap. Kids can really drive you crazy, you know, but man, they're worth it."

LaMarr launches into "the story of me and Kim's lives," now and then trying to draw his wife into the conversation. Kim, born in 1956, finally struggles up from the couch, trying not to wake the sleeping eight-month-old, returning on exaggerated tiptoe a few minutes later holding up crossed fingers. The couple were married in L.A. and went to Disneyland for their honeymoon. "I was wrestlin' with this big bottle of champagne on our weddin' night. I had a little trouble because of my arm not workin' and I twisted it and the cork flew out of the bottle and hit me back up on the head! I had a big lump!"

LaMarr, born in 1962, works at Cedars-Sinai Hospital in Los Angeles. "I clean toilets and bathrooms and stuff. It's not the greatest job, but the people there are real nice."

Couples with children have to work together to be good parents, LaMarr says. "You gotta be willin' to love each other and talk your problems out and share work, share everything."

LaMarr: I went to this special school in Highland Park and it was called the California Learning Center and they had these apartments where you could be independent and they teach you that. I went there and a friend introduce me to Kim. She was layin' on the couch watchin' TV. We were talkin' after and we had breakfast together and we walk to school together and from then on, we just been together.

What happen was that we graduate from this program and our counsellor at the Regional Center told us about this apartment in Glendale. We live there for six years. She lived upstairs with a friend and I live downstairs by myself. I would go upstairs and see her a lot all the time and she'd come down and see me, too, so finally we just wanted to get married. I ax her. I don't really remember how I did it. I just ax her to marry me and she was spectacle at first, but then she said yes. We got married in 1987.

Kim: Goin' on six years. March 14.

LaMarr: And we had Kevin, but then we couldn't live there cause they didn't allow kids so we hadda move. We hadda move out and we live with my mom for awhile.

Kim: Honey, we lived another place, too, before.

LaMarr: Oh, that's right. There was one place we lived that was a bad area. It was scary.

Kim: (wrinkles her nose) Not so scary. Just a lot of violence.

LaMarr: Yeah, I almost got, well, killed. Threatened anyways. We were coming home from a friend's and I stayed in the cab to watch the friend's little boy while the cab driver and Kim and the friend went upstairs to get money. And a Mexican came along and I could see him comin' in the mirror and he got in the cab. He threatened me; he said "Get out." Well, he didn't say it exactly like that. Worse. I don't want to say just how he said it, but it wasn't very nice. Like a fool, I say "What do you want?" He just yell "Get out, get out," so what I did was get out, but I got the little boy out before the man could take the car. He drove off. So we move out of there into my mom's. It's not easy livin' with your mom, so it was up and down.

Kim: (slaps her knee) Kevin, put that box of candy down, honey.

LaMarr: My mom, I really can't say how she felt about us livin' together. I think she was kinda worried. Cause she didn't think I could live on my own, you know. I told the whole family I was gettin' married. My mom was worried. My sister, she was a little worried, too. My brother and my dad, they were happy.

I hadn't really had other girlfriends before. Well, girlfriends in high school, you know. Kim was fun to be with. She still is, even after two kids. She's still fun cause when we found out she was pregnant, I was so excited. I'll tell you a story. We decided to have a family and Kevin, he was the first one. She took the home pregnancy test. It came out positive. We went to the doctor and he did a test and it was negative. So we weren't too happy. He told us to just keep tryin'. Next time, we try and Kim says she's feelin' the, you know, symptoms. I told her I'd go to the doctor with her after work, but by the time I get home, she was gone. I think she has went to the doctor, so I ran all the way there. When I ran, I got so tired. I ran right into the doctor office and then I fell down and almost broke a lamp off a table. The doctor said, "Calm down, LaMarr. You're gonna be a father." I told her, "No way, you must be lyin'!" She said "No, I'm not lyin'." I ran all over the hospital, yellin' "I'm gonna be a father! I'm gonna be a daddy!" I told everybody. I mean *everybody*!

We did the Lamaze classes. A person work with us. It was interesting because Kim had a baby shower. My father told me I'd never last five minutes in the delivery room, but I proved him wrong. I stayed for the *whole* thing. Didn't bother me at all. It was fun. Well, fun on my part, not on her part!

———

Kim: That's for sure. (raises her voice slightly) Kevin, honey, put that broom back in the kitchen and give me that box of candy. . . .

———

LaMarr: When I saw him first when the doctor held him up, cryin' and all, I just thought "What a beautiful life." It was just, you know, he's a beautiful baby. He's great.

We had some people tell us we shouldn't have a baby, you know. But they don't seem to understand it's not their choice, you know. It's ours. Our family was tellin' us just to have one. One child, because it's a lot of work and money. But I always wanted to not have an only child, but have a little brother or sister for Kevin. We thought about it. Every time our family said we should only have one, I'd listen but I knew it was my choice. I didn't want to argue with them. I'd just listen but in my heart I knew it was my choice. And Kim's. We decided a year before we had Baby Trevor, we decided to have another one.

Kim: (holds up three fingers on each hand) Kevin's name is Kevin Michael Johnson and Trevor's name is Trevor Anthony Johnson. My family was happy for me, you know. But it was hard breakin' the news. They were worried, you know, because LaMarr is handicapped and they didn't know how he'd help me with the kids. We just told them this is what we were gonna do. We're adults and I love LaMarr and LaMarr loves me and that's it. (Sternly) Kevin, put that box of candy down. That's my Valentine's present from La-Marr. A two-pound box of chocolates.

I loved LaMarr from the first time we met. It just grew as we got to know each other and we walk to school every day. When we wanted to get married, my mom was very ill. My mom died in 1985. She had cancer, so we waited until later to get married. My dad thought we should wait awhile, but when I got pregnant, he said, "Well, that's nice." He was more worried when I got pregnant again. You know, our parents worry a bit extra and he wondered where the money was gonna come from.

You gotta be willin' to love each other even when you have problems and be willin' to talk it out when problems arises. Kevin, put that down, honey (Kevin giggles).

LaMarr: You gotta have, you know, respect for your spouse. You have to help each other whenever you can and share work, share everything. Just love each other and try to work it out as best you can. We fight about stupid things, I can tell you that! We fight about TV, you know, what to watch. I *love* basketball. Kim, she says she likes basketball but she really doesn't cause when I watch the Lakers, she goes to bed.

Kim: (laughs) LaMarr, I go to bed cause I have the kids all day. When LaMarr's at work all day, I just get worn out and I have to get up early the next morning.

LaMarr: And I try to buy a lot of collectors items because my hero and my, you know, idol is Magic Johnson. My sister bought me some basketball cards and she got me the Olympics cards. Every time I see something about Magic Johnson, I just want it. I have his Laker jersey in my closet that I'm going to frame. I think he is the greatest basketball player that ever live. I was at a friend's house and when I came back home, Kim told me to call my sister cause me and my sister are both Lakers fans. So I did and she told me to watch TV when they was sayin' Magic had AIDS. I just cried. I watched it all night and I just cried. Kim tried to talk to me and I was too upset to even talk to her. I knew Magic was gonna die. My sister came over and that night we wrote a letter to Magic. I like Magic even more than Michael Jordan. AIDS and that stuff never cross my mind until I heard about Magic. But now I would never do something, you know, anybody can catch, like, diseases and you can learn to be careful. I wish Magic was careful. Yesterday, a little girl came up to me and ax me what happen to my arm (shorter and un-derdeveloped). I didn't know what to say, so I just went on about my business. I should have answer her. I wish I did. I play basketball every week at the Westside Community Center and those guys don't look at me like I'm handicapped.

Kim: (struggles up from the couch) Kevin. Kevin, what are you doin'? Put that back. LaMarr, can you get him? I used to work at Goodwill Industries. I used to work at a handicraft shop for handicapped people. You know, I think Kevin needs a nap.

LaMarr: When we had dated a while, I remember, I ax her to marry me and she turned me down. She wanted to live together for awhile. Before, the priest didn't want us to, you know, fool around before. But, you know, we didn't go by his rules. But then, she *told* the priest! (rolls his eyes) I guess I knew I was marryin' an honest person. The priest told us to forgive our sins, you know, and I hadda become a Catholic before we got married.

When it come down to the wedding, we got married at 12 o'clock. We ax my brother to be my best man. When the wedding came, I was talkin' to my brother, you know, like brother to brother, before she came down the aisle. He told me he always knew I would be a family man. When Kim came down the aisle, I had butterflies in my stomach. It was, like, scary. Kim says she was cryin' because she didn't want to leave her father. But we got through the ceremony and when we finish, we went outside and took pictures. The butterflies were gone then. My sister took us to the Disneyland Hotel for our honeymoon. It was nice. They had a TV. The bedroom was fun (he stutters), I mean, what I mean is, they had a basket of fruit and champagne. It was hard for me to open the champagne bottle with my arm and all and when I finally twisted it open, the cork flew up on the wall and hit me back up on the head!

Kim: (cups her son's face in her hands) Kevin, don't hit. That's not nice. Be a good boy now while Daddy's talkin'. Listen to Daddy talk about our honeymoon. And your brother is sleepin'; you have to be quiet.

LaMarr: Excuse me a minute. Now, Kevin, you gotta settle down. Boy, are you actin' up today.

This is the hard part about raisin' kids, I'm not kiddin'. When they want to be loud and the other one is posed to be sleepin'. You have to be very patient, you know. Anyway, Kim and me had fun. They even had an ocean right in the back.

Anyway, I work at Cedars-Sinai. I clean bathrooms. I work in the radiology area. And the X-ray area. I have a lot of people, even though I'm busy, I just talk to people for a few minutes, then I just get back to my work. My boss says they like me and they think I'm very nice. It's not really what I want to do, but it's a job and I'm just hangin' in there. I've worked at the hospital almost a year now and it's very nice. It's a drag when you get paid only once a month, though.

Kim: (nods) Yeah, a drag. It's hard to stretch the money you have. I get food stamps and we got a little money for the kids twice a month, but it's hard. There's some money for people who are disabled that have kids.

LaMarr: We try to shop smart, you know. Meat, vegetables . . .

Kim: Milk, bread.

LaMarr: We try to stay away from things that cost a lot. Like baby food. (laughs) No, I'm just kiddin'. She makes a shoppin' list and we get the stuff that's on the list. But, here, this is what makes me mad! Kim writes down what she's posed to write down and she ends up with stuff what's on the list and a few more stuff what's not on the list! That's more money! Then we get to the cash register and it's way more! I keep tellin' her just buy what's on the list, but she thinks of other stuff, too.

You know, we go shopping but we go most of the time for the kids. My sister and my mom are the greatest persons in the world. They help us out as much as they can. On Saturday, my sister come over and she get Kevin and Trevor's pictures taken and then we went to McDonald's to get somethin' to eat and after that we went to Graumann's Chinese Theatre and we see Michael Jackson's star on the Hollywood Boulevard. It's real fun and it don't cost nothin'! We got back late and order pizza. They really help us out a lot. We really appreciate everything they do. See, my mom, she comes sometimes and what I'm trying to do is get my own car instead of havin' my mom always come here. She live in Inglewood and I don't want her to put herself out all the time and be on the streets. If I can get a car, we can come over and visit her, too. My sister live in Westwood and that's not so bad.

Kim: LaMarr is very helpful around the house and with the kids. Sometimes he tells me to "Sit down and relax, Kim, I'll sweep the floor." But that's not the way I am. I just get up.

LaMarr: You know, at night, when the baby's cryin', I get up and I put him to sleep so Kim don't have to get up. When he is sick, then we . . .

Kim: Then we both get up when he's sick.

LaMarr: We both try to keep him occupied and give him his medicine. It's rough havin' kids, but it's enjoyable because they're so much fun. You know, when Kim was pregnant again and I helped her out and her Lamaze teacher came over to do all the breathing and the whole thing, so when it was time for Kim to go to the hospital, I stay with her the night. I help her out with her breathin', but when she had labor pains, she cried. I did, too, because I felt so bad that I put her through this pain again.

But now this is a funny story. Lemme tell you this! With Trevor, I'm tryin' to help the girl out, you know, using my breathing and stuff and she be tellin' me to shut up! She's yellin' at me what did I do this for? She was cussin' me out and pushin' me away. She's holdin' on to the nurse instead of me! When it was all over, and the doctor's holdin' the baby, I came over and she push me away and is huggin' the nurse! Man! She got her tubes tied after that one, lemme tell you!

Don and Brenda Thibault, son Trevor

Tisdale, Saskatchewan

W hen Brenda Thibault got bored in the hostel after the birth of son Trevor in the spring of 1987, she thought if she told someone she had slapped the baby, the nuns would get angry and send her and the infant home. They did get angry, but what happened to the Thibault family then wasn't at all what Brenda had anticipated. Although Brenda immediately recanted her story, it set in motion a family services apprehension of the baby, followed by a court custody battle. Brenda, 28, and husband Don, 41, eventually won, but the crisis-intervention theme was set and the custody of their son hangs by a thread.

Brenda, born in 1965, says she was "spoiled and never had to do nothing but watch TV" while she lived at home, met Don when she stopped at the local sheltered workshop to use the bathroom. "He showed me where it was," she smiles, talking in a hushed voice. Trevor is napping. Don, born in 1952, spent "10 or 13 years or in between 12 and 16" years in Valley

View Centre, a provincial institution in Moose Jaw, before moving to Tisdale, a small rural community, in 1975.

Brenda: We saw the minister for about a month before we got married. He told us we were going to run into a lot of walls because we're both slow learners, but he said if we were still sure, we could go ahead. I figured I have run into lots of walls growin' up in my life. We'll just show 'em we can.

I wasn't really nervous for my weddin' because I knew that's what I wanted to have. My dad died in 1983 and my mom came and my aunt and Don and his mom and sister was there. We had a lot of friends but in a small town everybody goes to all the weddin's and when I invite some people to the dance, the first thing they ask was "Will there be any alcohol?" When I said no, then they said they didn't know if they could make it.

(Brushes crumbs from her shirt) A lot of people told me Don was too old for me, but I don't care about that. I says as long as he loves me and treats me right, that's the best I'm gonna get. If that's what I get, his age shouldn't have nothin' to do with it.

I know I want to have children ever since I was little. We was married three years before I got pregnant. We been goin' together for nine years, so it wasn't like Don had to get to know me. It was a little hard at first to do chores and that cause I guess I was a little spoiled livin' at home with my mom cause she did everything. I hadda pull up my socks.

Don: (pushes his glasses up on his nose) It was kind of hard because I was doin' everything and I kept tellin' Brenda you have to help me around here. She'd get mad and say I was bossin' her around. But I was workin' so I couldn't do all the chores at home, too.

Brenda: When I had Trevor, I went in to Saskatoon and stayed there with him at Martha House. I told Sister Margaret I hit him cause I thought if I told her that, they'd let us go home. I missed Don and they were makin' me stay there. I went home all right, but they kept the baby. Trevor finally came to Tisdale, but we weren't allowed visiting rights on him. We ask if we could start seein' him, but the foster parents hadda bring him here. We couldn't ever see him alone. It was real hard.

The first thing they said was I hadda start lookin' after the house on my own. Don and me couldn't change Trevor, he couldn't feed him, he couldn't bath him. At times they told Don he wasn't allowed to touch him. What finally happen was I had a temper tantrum. I think any normal person would have a temper tantrum. I stayed at Don's mother's awhile to learn how to do things. But that was not good because they liked to play jokes on me. The worst was when she strip me naked 'cept for my bra and panties and locked me outside in broad daylight. And then she took a picture of me, then she strip me bare naked and told me to go answer the door. I told her I might be stupid but she was more mental than me if she expect me to go answer the door with no clothes on. She told me not to call her mental or she'd make me sorry and I decided no way was I gonna stay there anymore. I don't know why she did those things, but I know she didn't like me very much. They thought maybe I'd leave Don if they were mean to me long enough. She'd yell at me "Get off your big fat ass" and do whatever she wanted. It wasn't very nice at all.

Don: (quietly looks into his coffee cup) My mom and sister would meet me different places and call Brenda all kinds of names to get me to leave her.

Brenda: I left there and I come back here and I told the welfare people there was no way I could stay there. At times I felt that people didn't care. I'd tell them and they wouldn't do nothin'.

    The foster family had lotsa rules about Trevor. I always like to rock him to sleep and the lady said she didn't want him to expect her to do that, so I wasn't supposed to cuddle him so much. They had sent in people to our house who were supposed to teach us how to work with Trevor and look after him. But they just sat there and write notes. After a few months, they start to really help us and wrote in their reports that we were doin' a good job and would be good parents if we had some help. Then the welfare people pulled those people out. I think they decide all along that we shouldn't have Trevor, so it don't matter how good we learned. We'd never get him. I think the only reason we was able to fight for Trevor was that my mom died in 1987 and she left me a lot of money. So we got a lawyer. And if we didn't have that money, I don't think we woulda got Trevor.

Don: I had to lay down the law with Brenda and told her if she didn't start growin' up and lookin' after some things, we'd never see Trevor again. That seem to do some good. That scare her. She's still trying.

Brenda: I said to Don I really want Trevor and I said to myself I better straighten up. I felt sometimes they was holding Trevor out in front of us like a present if we done a good job, but they were never going to give him back anyways. No matter what I did, I felt like I couldn't please them all.

Don: We felt we were ganged up on. We were tryin' to do somethin' right. We never knew when different workers were goin' to show up or what time. One worker would tell us to do one thing, so we would and then another would say, "No, you can't have Trevor until you do that another way."

Brenda: (twirls her finger by her ear) To tell ya the truth, I felt in my mind I was goin' nuts. One day we were runnin' late and Don said let's just take Trevor to the cafe for lunch today before we take him back to the foster home. We never had him alone; the Home Care lady was with us. But it was busy in the cafe and we ended up bein' a half an hour late. The foster lady sent her husband out lookin' for us. They thought we took off with him. Kidnap him like.

The social workers would come and ask questions and write stuff down. I might as well go back to school, I felt like I was takin' a test all the time. The Home Care ladies said they felt it was all silly and that too many people were comin' and goin'. It was like they were all just waitin' for us to make a mistake.

Don: (pours more coffee) The hardest part was always having so many people here from social services and that, sorta watching us to see if we made a mistake. (Brenda pushes away from the table and returns with a plate of banana bread.) They wrote down that Brenda didn't put some food back in the fridge, and another time she left a butter knife on the kitchen counter. They said that was dangerous for Trevor. That didn't seem fair.

Brenda: I've had to learn a lot of things. I had to learn to not be lazy and help Don with the house and the baby. It was real hard, but Don was always there for me and he kept sayin' I could do it.

Don: Then we decided to go to court and the war started. We hadda collect what the lawyer said was called evidence.

Brenda: When we went to court, I knew I hadda tell the truth. I didn't lie because I knew you can't lie in court, even if I could have made me look better. If you lie, you're in a lot of trouble. They ask me if I know what takin' a oath means and I told 'em it means you can't lie.

    The judge was a very nice man and he was real easy to talk to. He could be very strict but he was never mean to us. I had never been in court on a stand before in my life, so I was a little nervous. I was surprised when that other lawyer, like the opposition guy, would ask me somethin', then he'd talk about somethin' else, then he'd ask me that same question again, but a little different. So he was trying to trip me up and make me change my answer. But our lawyer said that's what he'd do, so I was ready for it. When he did that, I just said, "Like I said before . . . ," so he didn't get me! Don was real good, too. I think it's important in court that you gotta dress up and show everybody that you do care about the way you look. That you really care, because in court, we had to show how much we care about everything. God musta been watchin' us.

Don: (smiles proudly) I went out and got my driver's license. I kept puttin' it off, but I finally realize we had a two-year-old and how far can a two-year-old walk, or you carry him, especially in wintertime.

Brenda: When the judge finally made his decision announcement in court, we didn't understand what he meant. Our friend Doreen was trying to explain it. She knew Don from a long time ago when he live at Valley View Centre and she work there. We just couldn't believe it. The judge was supposed to tell us on the 21st and then he said he wanted to wait until the 28th. They kept tellin' me they won't take Trevor away, they won't take Trevor away. I just cried. Then it was worth all the work Don and me and the Home Care ladies done and they turned into our very good friends.

Don: We will still have some problems, but we can learn and we want to be good parents for our little boy. We have to try not to argue and fight. We feel proud because we learned a lot and we learned we can call people for help.

Brenda: But we learn we can't expect people to do things for us all the time. If we want to keep Trevor, we have to work hard. To me, Number One, I was abused by a foster child in our home and I don't want that to ever happen to my baby. One thing I really remember that I learn was when I was makin' supper and Trevor came along and hug my leg and held his arms up. The Home Care lady said to stop what I was doin' and pay attention because Trevor want a hug. That was the first time he ever done that. Usually he went to Don. I was so happy he done that.

(Tears well in her eyes) At first I almost felt uncomfortable around him when we only had him a few hours a day. I didn't want to get too close to him cause I couldn't imagine what it would hurt like when they took him away for good.

The one person I could really count on in the court bad times was Don. He was strong and he kept tellin' me "Don't worry, we'll get him back" even though he probably didn't think we might. I think the best decision I ever made, besides havin' Trevor, was marryin' my husband Don.

———————

Don: (pushes glasses up on his forehead and wipes his eyes) See, I told you I couldn't do any better.

Update: In the summer of 1993, Don and Trevor moved to a room and board home in Regina, Saskatchewan, following a separation from Brenda. "I'm going to try to do my best for Trevor," Don says. "We can go for a walk and bike ride and I will get up in the morning and get him ready for school. I took Trevor and went to library and got some books for Trevor and I to read. We take the bus to the library and doctor office. He doesn't ask about Brenda. The Lord has something planned for me down the line," Don says. "He just says to hold on." Don's parenting is supported by the family in the home. Brenda continues to live in Tisdale and now attends the local sheltered workshop and, says Don, has seen Trevor only once since the separation.

Ron and
Hazel Neal, son Louis

Estevan, Saskatchewan

$\mathcal{F}$ or Ron and Hazel Neal, 1992 and 1993 were tough years.
Several months after their wedding on October 26, 1991,
Hazel complained to her doctor of weight gain and a chronic
upset stomach. The doctor prescribed a diet and anti-nausea
medication; Hazel continued to take her epilepsy medication
and birth control pills. When someone suggested to the director of their independent living program that Hazel might be
pregnant, the reaction was one of disbelief. No pregnancy
test was ever done. Several months later, a frightened and
confused Hazel went into labor, a development that con-
vinced people she was pregnant. Baby Louis was born in
June 1992 with a cleft lip and palate and heart problems,
and spent almost the first full year of his life in the hospital. Cor-
rective surgery just before his first birthday was successful and
he finally was able to live at home with his parents. Hazel, 34,
and Ron, 36, receive live-in support from Social Services and
they look forward to the day when Louis can eat and drink
through his mouth instead of through a tube in his nose. The
support workers teach and assist, but are firm in their belief

that "Louis is *their* baby and they need the chance to learn to take care of him."

Caring for their son is the couple's greatest concern. Their strength has been tested; Ron's mother died in March 1992, his father in April 1993, and Hazel's father died in January 1993. Through it all, Ron, born in 1957, has kept his job with SaskOil, driving to oil drill sites to maintain the grounds. "I don't want to go back to the sheltered workshop," he says firmly. "You don't make no money there. Hazel's not going back either. And Louis will never go there if we have anything to say about it." The couple has matured in significant ways; with a new air of confidence, Hazel, born in 1959, recently returned to her doctor and insisted all her family's health records be transferred to the new physician in town. Within days, her new doctor made a house call to meet Hazel and Ron and welcome Baby Louis to her practice.

Ron: How it started, okay, at the time I was down in the dumps and she saw me at the mall. She said she'd buy me a coffee. My girlfriend had left me and I told Hazel all about it.

Hazel: I knew him. We both work at the shop at that time. He look so sad so I buy him coffee and he talk to me.

Ron: We been goin' steady ever since. We started talkin' about gettin' married. By the time I got engage with her, it was very romantic, it was. It was nice. I ask her "Do you want to marry me?" She wasn't too sure yet. Then later, I didn't have the ring yet til I knew each other better first then I buy her a ring. I had to surprise her at the time so I went out and got it. It wasn't easy to give it to her. I said, "Close your eyes and open the box." She said, "What is it?" and I said, "I'm not gonna tell you."

Hazel: I didn't know what it was. I was shocked. I put it on right away on my finger. When I got married, I hadda take it off. It was a lot of work for my wedding. My dress was homemade. . . . It's time to feed Louis. I gotta hook him up. Ron, you tell the story. Sometimes (smiles broadly) I call Louis "Nuisance."

Ron: We got married in Estevan. October, yeah. I was nervous. I was. I can say I was, yes. Both times. Before and after.

Hazel: (Hooks up the bag of formula on the machine that feeds Louis through his nasal tube) When we got married and then we got sick together. We got food poisoning.

After a while, I wasn't feeling good for a long time so I went to the doctor and she gave me some medicine. I don't know I was having a baby. Even my parents didn't know. I felt something funny in my stomach, and I tell the doctor I don't feel good. I was throwing up and the doctor gave me medicine for that. After awhile I got bad pains and they took me to the hospital and he was born. It was a big surprise to everybody. I was in shock. They let us see him right away. He was with the other babies. They tell us what was wrong with his mouth and they said they can fix it. They took him away to Regina. I stay with him in Regina a lot, but Ron hasta stay here to work.

Ron: We name him Louis, how we done that it was after my mother's name. Her name was Annie Mary Louise, so we took the E off and got Louis. His whole name is Louis David. The best thing is to have him at home now instead of Regina.

Hazel: He likes Barney, you know, the dinosaur. Don't you, Louis? He has a little toy Barney and he bites the head.

Ron: He sleeps until about three in the morning and then he wakes up. I go in and check on him to see if he's okay. He sleeps pretty good. Sometimes he doesn't like the tube in his nose.

   I was out at work in the oil patch when a guy come out and told me I was going to be a father. I got so excited, I couldn't believe it. On the way back to town, I got a flat tire. Oh, boy! I couldn't believe it.

Hazel: That's true, he couldn't believe it. I had pains off and on and all the time. I thought I had the flu and then a doctor came along and told me I was gonna have a baby. A friend of mine hadda go back home and get my suitcase and some clothes. I had a Caesarian.

Ron: I had to make my own suppers while she was in the hospital. I was all in shock. I pretty near fell over. I wasn't in the room cause it was an operation, but right away I got to hold him. He was small.

Hazel: He had lots of hair on his head.

Ron: (laughs) Yeah, plenty of hair. Lots. Reddish like mine when I was a baby.

Hazel: I was worried about his mouth, but the whole thing was such a shock.

Ron: And they show me where there were two spots in his heart that aren't closed. They have to close them up in Saskatoon when he's about three, I think. Right, Louis? Look, here's your Barney.

Hazel: He didn't like the tube in his nose at first. Before the operation, he could put his finger in his mouth and pull everything out. I was runnin' to the hospital a lot so they could put it back in. But not no more.

Ron: We got some help, me and Hazel. They help us feed Louis through his tube. Hazel knows how to hook him up to the machine. We do it and they show us now.

Hazel: We're gonna have early intervention teacher, too. They bring toys. We couldn't at first because he was in Regina at the hospital so much. But now he's home for good and we can start teaching him things. We want him to learn to drink from the bottle and not have the tube no more. I don't want him to have the tube all his life.

Ron: Time and patience. That's all it takes. We just keep working. Louis, you dropped Barney, didn't ya? Dad will get it for you. He likes his bath. He lays there and kicks and laughs. He laughs all the time.

Hazel: He likes green beans. And butterscotch.

Ron: (pats Louis's cheek) He likes food in his mouth now after his operation. He likes cereal, too. And carrots. Not raw carrots, he's too little. Pablum carrots he likes.

Hazel: You get used to routine and it's not too hard. We love him and Virginia and Kathy help us learn what to do. They don't do it for us. We do it because we're Louis's mom and dad.

Ron: I still work for SaskOil. I cut weeds for leases. I get up at five o'clock in the morning, sometimes 4:30. Long hours and a lot of driving, but it's good money. Better than the workshop. Oh, yeah, a lot better. I want to keep doing it. If I went back to the shop again, I won't make enough money for us as I can outside. I'm old fashioned that way, but I don't wanna go back.

Hazel: I was at the workshop for a long time. When I had Louis, I quit and never went back since. They ask me back to work on buttons, but no way. I want to stay with Louis. Is that a good idea, Louis? Maybe when he's in school, I'll get a good job like washing dishes in a cafe, but I'm not goin' back to the shop. I was even thinkin' about goin' back to school, maybe to college.

Louis had two different haircuts already. One in the hospital and one for his baptism.

I was takin' small white pills so I wouldn't get pregnant. I didn't know I was pregnant so I just kept takin' them. I switch doctors after. I did it myself. She's a nice lady. She even came over to our house to meet Ron and Louis. I like her better. She tells me the proper things and she talks to me more than the other one done. She got two kids of her own, too.

Ron is a really good dad. Really good. He plays with Louis and he gives him juice and that. He help out around with housework.

Ron: What we do is if we ever have a argument is like this. Well, we . . .

Hazel: Go out and have some fresh air! (laughs)

Ron: If she's inside, then I go outside and go for a walk until I say okay, my temper's all gone and I come back in and talk.

Hazel: Sometimes we argue about not keepin' the house tidy enough.

Ron: Sometimes I have only my way, sometimes we have only her way. It's hard to give up your way even if you know it's not right. That's very hard, but you have to share ways.

(quietly) I lost both my parents this year. I lost my own folks and my father-in-law, too.

Hazel: I lost my dad on my side. It's been a very hard year for us.

Ron: It was rough. It wasn't easy. It was not easy. I don't like to talk about it too much. I just can't. It's too soon. . . . (covers his face with his hands and breathes deeply).

Hazel: (brightly) Our anniversary is comin' up! It'll be two years. Lots happen in two years, right, Ron? We got Louis. I would tell people who say I can't have a baby it's my choice and not theirs. We can do it. It's not that hard. We can manage. If we didn't have no help, we could still manage just the two of us. I think I'll put Louis in his crib. He's gettin' pretty tired cause he's rubbin' his eyes. He likes his bath, then he gets sleepy. And cranky. (lifts Louis from his bassinet in the center of the table). Come on, Buddy. Bedtime.

Ron: I like bein' a dad. The best thing is proud. The first time I bein' a father for a whole year now. Had my first Father's Day in June, too. Hadda work on my Father's Day, believe it or not! He was in the hospital for Mother's Day. I missed Hazel and Louis when they were in Regina. They were there a long time, but I can't lose too much time off work. I worry about that. If I go any place without special permission, I get my check docked. No pay. That's not good. Keep on workin' is good, but I hadda take one day to go see Louis on his first birthday. I got pay docked, but it was important.

One thing what I crossed my mind when he was born is that Louis might not make it. I keep tellin' myself and I keep tellin' Hazel, "He's gonna make it. He's gonna make it." The doctors didn't know even. He was five pounds, and three quarter ounce. (Calls to the bedroom) Hazel, do you need any help? Okay, I'll come in.

In the future, I think from there he might go to college. I would like that very much. Maybe a carpenter. No, not that. Maybe a engineer. No, not that. Maybe a mechanic. I don't want him to ever work at the shop, I don't want to see him there. I don't want him to work there and make less money like what we went through. Cripes, yes. I don't want that for him. Cripes, no (tiptoes into the baby's room).

Hazel: (lifts Louis up so Ron can brush his hair) I want to have more kids, but they was always buggin' me to get my tubes tied, this lady in town. I said no so many times, but they was always tellin' me I hadda do it. I couldn't stand the pressure no more. I went to a school for just people with handicaps and they always tell us what to do. It was boring and sickening. Nothin' to do. You couldn't go anywhere without your parents. They pen us in. I don't

like to think about it no more. I didn't like it. High school was good.
I really like it. It wasn't a special school. But some kids tease me
and givin' me a hard time, but I just ignore them altogether. I got a
relation in the same class as me so I feel really good about that then.

We went out for coffee, just me and Ron awhile ago and we pay
Virginia and Kathy what we would pay a babysitter. We went for
coffee and we call home to see how Louis is and he was fussy so we
come home. That's what you gotta do when you're a mom.

Ron: Our parents were really proud of him. My brother is really
good to us and he lets us make our own decisions, but he helps us.

Hazel: Sometimes people tell us to go to Special Olympics and
that, even if we don't want to they say we have to. They think it's
for real and it's posta just be for fun. And all of us from the shop
went camping and I ask if I could work in the kitchen and they said
no, I hadda be with the other handicapped people. I was really hurt
by that cause I wanted to work there.

Ron: They think a person's handicapped and they think this and
that, so I don't know what the deal is. Before I met Hazel, I said to
this other girl's mom, "Can I see your daughter?" and the mother
said no because she is fully handicapped. She only had one arm,
too, and her mother said I couldn't marry her because she could
never handle a kid.

Hazel: (frowns) People told me that, too. They always tell us
we're retarded or whatever and I don't like that word. I hate that. I
would say about myself a person can do lots of things like cleanin'
and cookin' and shoppin' and they're not retarded. I don't like that
word at all.

Ron: We knew our marriage would work out good. We take it step by step. We went out to supper only with my mom just before the wedding. She told me . . . (swallows and closes his eyes). She told me she been married all her life and . . . (struggles to avoid tears) . . . she told me I could do it. . . . Geez, I just can't talk. I miss her.

Hazel: (smiles at her husband) We want to stay here for always. When Louis gets more older, we won't be havin' no help no more. We do it ourselves. I hope the tube in Louis' nose can be gone by Christmas and he can learn to eat and drink in his mouth. If I could have anything, that will be our Christmas gift to Louis. In a way it's nice to have Kathy and Virginia now while we're learnin', but someday it will be just us. Our family.

Update: In early 1994, baby Louis was placed in an approved private service home through the Family Services Act Section Nine. Because of continuing medical complications and the seriousness of the interventions required, stress became a major factor not only for Ron, Hazel, and their baby, but also for the care providers. Questions were raised about the cost of providing such intensive support to one family, and a meeting was called. Several options were discussed, including shared parenting. At least for the time being, Louis will live with his parents one-third of each month and in the approved private services home for two-thirds. The woman who came forward to become Louis's foster mother is

Virginia, the live-in care provider who has been with the Neal family since Louis came home from the hospital.

Though Hazel has had some pressure to go back to the sheltered workshop to curb her loneliness, Deb Hagel, an employment counselor, is working with her to find a job in the community. "These parents have faced a situation over the past year and a half that would be mind-boggling for any family," says Hagel. "The future's a little uncertain right now, especially in terms of Louis's health, but we need to work on a way in which the Neal family unit is respected. To go in and just remove Louis would be a tragedy for everyone concerned. They're good parents who've had to deal with more than their share of stress and hardship and they've come through. A little ragged maybe, but they've come through."

Shane and Brenda Haddad, son Tyler

Regina, Saskatchewan

$\mathcal{T}$ aking a break from studying the assembly directions for his stationary exercise bike, Shane, 30, rests his meaty arms on the kitchen table. Brenda, 29, who seems tailor-made for the expression "90 pounds soaking wet," places a steaming cup of instant coffee before him. In a sing-song voice, he teases: "Thank you, Brenda, you take such good care of your hus band." She returns to the table with their wedding album under one arm and three-year-old son Tyler under the other arm. Their wedding was an elaborate affair in the spring of 1989. Tyler was born a year later.

The couple are outspoken members of the self-advocacy organization People First; Shane is the president of the provincial council, Brenda is the secretary. They are frustrated with people who don't respond as quickly as they'd like to the involvement of people with disabilities, particularly on volunteer boards. "Why should we have to campaign to get elected? They should see we deserve to have a voice, you know, on the board." Brenda nods vigorously and retrieves a toy for Tyler as it rolls under the table. "That's right, Shane. You tell

'em, dear," she says in the same sing-song. His anger dis-
sipates and he chuckles.

Reaching for his son, who giggles and spits, Shane speaks
in baby-talk, "Youse wanna come to your Daddy now?" then
to Brenda, he grins: "He's handsome. Just like his dad."

Shane: I seen her first. In 1983, I think it started when I was
playin' basketball for Special O and Brenda was there watchin' her
boyfriend. They had a big spat that night and she got real mad at her
boyfriend and that's when I met her at a house party.

Brenda: He was sorta goin' out with somebody else, but it musta
been love at first sight with little hearts in the air and everything!

Shane: Anyways, we went to movies and this and that. And this
one day when Brenda was around 21, her father grounded her. . . .

Brenda: For gettin' hammered and stayin' out late and stayin'
over at a man's house.

Shane: After that Brenda decided she wasn't a kid anymore
and . . .

Brenda: (waves her hand) So I moved out. A girlfriend had a
apartment already. Mom and Dad were totally against it because I'd
been sick and that. . . .

Shane: A year later, we decided to move in together at my place on Winnipeg Street. She was always over anyway and I guess we just fell madly in love. And I like the idea that you live together to make sure everything's right before . . .

Brenda: We got engaged before we moved in together. We went together to find a ring. We went to the pawn shop to see what they had and I seen this one I liked. He said, "Well, would you like that to be your engagement ring?" And I said, "Well, jeez, I don't know. I like it, so whatever!"

Shane: I think what sold her on the whole idea was when she saw the house on Winnipeg Street. She fell in love with the place right off. It had two bedrooms, a big living room and a big kitchen. We were both taking life skills classes then.

Brenda: After, we moved to Queen Street. That's when we decided to get married. When we first moved in together, my parents really hated it.

Shane: When we decided to get married, they hated it, too, because they felt Brenda should marry a rich person so she was taken care of okay. My mom and dad got to the point where they agreed to pay for the wedding, then Brenda's parents came around. It was pretty tense. My parents know what Brenda and I can accomplish and they know we're good for each other and we have determination.

Things got hotter and we were plannin' the marriage and we were going to Reverend Hart. To get marriage, we had to have marriage counselling and we talked about what problems and what we'd do. I think that's a very good idea because it teaches you to talk to each other about stuff.

Brenda: Just before we moved in together, I got real sick and lived at home with my mom and dad for awhile. They saw the ring on my finger and they freaked out. They didn't really like him and they figured I was too young. But I'm the baby in the family. My mom told my dad I was on birth control. My family was always worried I'd get in trouble with guys who didn't care about me. But I'm not dumb and I knew Shane was a decent guy.

The biggest thing I like about Shane right from when I first met him was he let me be myself. You know, me. Other guys would always try to get me to change and be the way they want. Shane was not into drugs and alcohol and parties and that's what I needed. And also when he found out he was a diabetic, he thought he was going to lose me. That I wouldn't stay with him. I told him "Big deal you're a diabetic." Even if he got cancer or something, I'd stay. You can't help stuff like that.

Shane: (whispers) About S-E-X. She was related to Virginia at that time, if you get it. That's a joke. It means she was a virgin.

Brenda: Shane was the first person I got, you know, involved with. I mean *really* involved with, you know . . .

Shane: Sexually. Just say it, Brenda!

Brenda: (sighs) Okay, sexually involved with. The other guys, I just went out to go out. I never really felt anything like that.

Shane: She even had one boyfriend who kicked her and injured her tailbone. He was over six feet tall and she's real little and she had to go for treatments. Nice guy.

Brenda: He asked me to get into bed with him and all that stuff but I said no way. I was pretty lucky, because he was really big and strong and I'm so little. I know people that guys don't even listen to when they say no and they can't do nothin' but wait till it's over.

Shane: I liked things about Brenda like her company and the way she express herself and like so many other girls after awhile would just mosey on down the road and you'd be heartbroken and everything else. But Brenda wasn't like that.

Brenda: I know girls who just use their man, you know, to get stuff and use their money. I'm not using him one bit. (laughs) He doesn't even have any money, so I can't use it anyways!

Shane: When we were living on her own and my own, we'd go out and share stuff. There are lots of girls who think it's a man's duty to pay for everything and Brenda and I took turns.

Brenda: When I moved out on my own, I had to go on welfare for awhile. When my parents found out, they didn't like that at all. My parents and I still argue quite a bit so we still don't see them very much. I have a lot of health problems, like my jaw problems and I get headaches, earaches. I'm looking into it, but getting my jaw fixed will cost a lot of money, but maybe the Kinsmen* will pay for it with Telemiracle** money. That's what they raise that money for, to help people fix stuff they can't afford to.

Shane: My bachelor party was at my best man's. It was a great party. We played horserace games. You roll the dice and move the horse the number on the dice. At the end, I got a Budweiser clock that worked, but doesn't work now. We got it on the wall for decoration. I went home after and it wasn't too much after that the wedding day was. The night before, I stayed alone. I wasn't nervous then. I started gettin' nervous at the church when the weddding party, you know, the girls were a little late.

Brenda: I had a girls' night out and a shower, too. The night he had his bachelor party, my sister and my girlfriend took me out to the bar and we got drunk. We went to my sister's. I wasn't nervous then. The night of my shower, my sister called and asked Shane and I to come over to visit. Shane knew what was going on, so he told me to dress nice. So we get to the door and went in and everybody was downstairs.

Shane: Anyways, when I saw her come down the aisle and all, I thought she was beautiful. My sister Tammy was not supposed to be

---

*   *Community service organization.*

** *Telethon.*

at the wedding because she was supposed to be in Yellowknife, way up north, but she surprised us and came.

We had drinks at our wedding that had flames on them. When we were at the reception and when it was time to throw her bouquet and when she threw it, it landed in the rafter. So I hadda get a ladder and go up and get it. When it came time to take off her garter, someone yelled out, "Shane, you look like you done this before!"

Brenda: One thing we're workin' on between Tyler and the next baby is our health. I want to get my jaw fixed (the jaw is not aligned properly) and put on some weight and get healthier and he (pokes him in the stomach) wants to take off some weight, right, Chubby Face? I don't think it's right when a man and a woman just keep havin' kids and don't think about it. We've talked about it a lot.

Another thing I'm workin' on is when we have arguments, I throw things and scream. We don't handle arguments the right way. Sometimes I worry a lot and my head gets dizzy and my stomach hurts. I get mad and I really throw things. I think when I get my jaw fixed it will help. When I was on my own a long time ago, I tried to commit suicide.

Shane: Brenda really has a wart on her shoulder about some things.

I got married with a semi-beard. Brenda says if I grow a beard, she's gonna leave me. But this semi-beard must be some kind of magnet for her. I think she likes hairy guys!

Brenda: If I get mad, he comes and hugs me and kisses me and brings me presents. (laughs) Maybe I should get mad more often!

Shane: If I was gonna give advice to anybody, I'd tell people if you think you can get married and handle the idea of becoming one, then don't forget to have respect for each other. We've had some really, really doozy arguments where her arms are goin' and everything and I'm just tryin' to hold her back. She's got to get used to me doin' things differently when there's somethin' bothering her and I want to be there to comfort her. When I try to comfort her, she bites me in the arm or whatever. That's my wife. She turns into the Terminator.

Brenda: (holds her fists in the air over her head) Sometimes I get so mad I don't know what to do. I tell him it's not him, but I can't stand it when he tries to hug me when I'm mad. One thing is very important if I'm mad is to pick up Tyler and some toys and put him in his bedroom and shut the door. He shouldn't be in the room if I'm upset because that's not good for him to see.

One important thing Shane does if I'm not happy is he'll say "Come on, we'll get a babysitter and we'll go somewhere just the two of us." At first I don't want to, but after I'm always glad so he's real smart that way. When we lived on Winnipeg Street, there was a hill not very far . . .

Shane: (smiles) This is real romantic.

Brenda: I know, so don't interrupt!

We always went to this hill and sat together in each other's arms and talk. So still today any time we have problems or just want to talk about us and Tyler and our lives, we just go there. And nobody knows about it, it's private.

Shane: When you have kids, the first concern is the kid (points to his son playing on the floor). For us, even if he bumps his head or is a little sick, you should still always call the doctor just in case you should bring the baby in. It just doesn't matter if it's 30 below outside. You still go start the car and warm it up for the baby. The thing I suggest is even if you're not workin', don't give up. Keep lookin' and do whatever you can to make money for your family. I've got a part-time job at the kids' home as a maintenance man and I deliver for Kentucky Fried Chicken and I've made about $400 shovelling snow this winter. A bunch of little jobs add up and makin' money is important.

Brenda: I've told a lot of people we know to quit smokin' and think of all the money they'd save. That's another reason I love Shane because he doesn't smoke. When we first met, he picked up a cigarette every once in awhile, I think just to be cool and impress me till he found out it just makes me sick instead.

Shane: If a couple has problems, they shouldn't be afraid to ask for help. It don't mean you're bad parents, but you gotta remember the bad part of it all is who gets hurt in the middle. Your kid. For us, it would be our little guy, our little buddy. Brenda goes to the Merichi Centre. It's a place for mothers and fathers and babies that need some extra help.

Brenda: (picks up her son from the floor) We got childhood intervention, too, and the lady comes in to our house and they show us how to work with him so he grows right and learns things the way he's supposed to.

Shane: (strokes the baby's head) Tyler's already been to swimming lessons. When he was four or five months old. We even got a certificate for it. He's gonna be very smart and hopefully he will go farther in his life than we are.

Update: The Haddads' second son was born February 17, 1994, weighing in at 7 pounds, 10 ounces. "I'm at home with Tyler while Brenda is in the hospital," says Shane. "We named him Matthew Ryan and he's 20 inches long. Tyler's been in to see him and he got to hold him and thinks it's pretty neat to have a brother. He looks just like Tyler, too. We would have liked a girl, and we're going to have to talk a lot about if we have another one or if this is it."

Tyler has started nursery school at nearby Sacred Heart School, and an early intervention teacher visits every two weeks.

THE BEST IS YET TO BE

We do not believe in ourselves until someone reveals that deep inside us something is valuable, worthy of listening to, worthy of our trust, sacred to our touch. Once we believe in ourselves, we can risk curiosity, wonder, spontaneous delight or any experience that reveals the human spirit.
— *e.e. cummings*

There is no medicine like hope, no incentive so great and no time so powerful as the expectation of something tomorrow.
— *O.S. Marsden*

Mary Boychuck and Victor Pickard

Assiniboia, Saskatchewan

S he unceremoniously adjusts her dentures and slurps her coffee while he pats her shoulder with a shaky hand. Victor, milky eyes crinkled at the corners, proudly surveys the dingy coffee shop as he drapes an arm around her shoulders. "My little honey. My little Mary," he murmurs, and she appears not to notice his fawning. She pulls the knitted cap from her head and rubs down her cropped grey hair. "Victor's awful nice," she says.

Victor, 77, beams at her. Mary, 62, suddenly struggles to her feet, jamming her cap back on her head. They begin their tour of this small rural farm town, leaning on each other to avoid slipping on snowy streets. Often she gets impatient and scurries ahead, leaving him to call for her as he brings up the rear. It is always the same. First, the coffee shop. Then a quick tour through downtown, where store clerks chat with them a few moments, then on to Kentucky Fried Chicken, where Victor buys Mary a chicken sandwich. He chats to her while she eats. Sometimes, he leans across the table to wipe her chin.

Mary spent 56 years in provincial institutions. Labelled a "behavior problem," she was often drugged or restrained or denied cigarettes as punishment for disobedience. Now, she lives with a family on a farm "where there's peace and quiet and nobody to fight with and I got me a pumpkin patch and I sell the pumpkins for a dollar. And I go for a walk every day without bein' told to." Victor, who lives in a seniors' apartment complex in town, and Mary speak of marrying one day, but are afraid of losing government benefits if they do. "We'll just have to wait and see," he says. "That would be real nice to marry Victor," Mary nods between mouthfuls. "I could take care of him and do his laundry cause he's real nice."

Victor: That Mary, she can find me anywhere when she comes to town lookin' for me (chuckles). Her nose starts itchin' when she thinks about me. Sometimes I buy my Mary some Cokes for her to take home.

Mary: Yup, he buy me some Cokes and one time he bought me an umbrella.

Victor: I got a little gold frame for a little picture of Mary and me. It's a real sweet picture of Mary and me kissin'. I think she looks real pretty in her new blue glasses. I like them glasses, they make her look real pretty.

Mary: (pushes her glasses up) If I get married to Victor, I would do his laundry and iron his shirts. I would look after him. He's a nice guy; a very nice guy. He loves me very much. Ho, ho, Victor is very nice. Anyways, he really likes me. Whenever I come to see him, he always buys me a chicken sandwich. He useta work at the salt mine; he did something there, I don't know what.

Victor: Oh gosh, yes, we are good friends. My little Mary. We been together quite a bit, haven't we, honey? I like to give Mary little presents, like a little picture of Mary and Jesus that I found in a rummage sale. I thought Mary would like that in her room at the farm.

Mary: Victor and me are goin' to Hawaii for our honeymoon when we get married. We're savin' our money cause it costs lots of money to go to Hawaii. It's warm there anyways. But we gotta wait cause if we get married before I am 65, then we don't get all our money. I hate to wait. If I was married to Victor, I could take care of him. He's a nice man. I don't smoke anymore and Victor don't smoke. I ask Esther if she thought I should quit smokin'. I coughed a lot. I smoked since I was nine; I started out in the bushes. I feel better and I don't stink. Victor says I smell nice.

Victor: She's a lovely woman, she sure is. When Mary and me walk around town, she takes my hand so I won't let her fall, but sometimes she walks so fast she gets ahead of me. When my nose gets itchy, I know Mary's thinkin' about me and my nose is itchy all the time!

Mary: I live with Esther and Charles and the boys on the farm and I got me a garden and every year I plant three rows of pumpkins and the whole damn thing come up! (laughs hard, then coughs. Victor reaches over to pat her shoulder). I sell the real big ones for two dollars and the small ones for one dollar. It's nice and peaceful at

Esther's. She has so many flowers and I go for long walks and I count gopher holes. There are 56 and 57 or 51. Lots. You gotta behave yourself and listen to what people tell you to stay out of the institution. I like bein' out. No one to touch my stuff, no one to fight with.

————————

Victor: (pats Mary's hand and reaches over with a napkin to wipe mayonnaise from her chin) My little honey.

————————

Mary: Yep, Victor and me are goin' to Hawaii. Sometimes he buys me Cokes. I like him a awful lot. A awful lot.

Gene "Hoppy" Sammons and Irene Lamb

Pukekohe, New Zealand

*W*earing a sleeveless cotton housedress and worn slippers, Irene, 59, surveys the rickety kitchen table, laden with several plates of sliced loaves and fancy biscuits.* Her deeply wrinkled face, sans teeth, creases into a smile as Hoppy, 68, shuffles into the dining room with the kettle. She holds the teapot steady as he pours. The two have been Platonic friends since the 1950s, when they both lived in Kingseat Hospital, a major psychiatric institution 60 kilometers from Auckland. Later, they lived together in the Raventhorpe Hospital, 54 kilometers from Auckland. This small rural facility was originally built by the U.S. Military during World War II for injured soldiers, but became a psycho-geriatric long-term care facility after the war. (Kingseat is scheduled to close in 1996; Raventhorpe was closed in May 1988 and all its residents were moved into the community.)

---

* *Cookies.*

After Raventhorpe closed, staff arranging Hoppy's and Irene's return to community living made sure the friends moved together. They first moved to a group home with other friends and finally to the house on Seventh Street in Pukekohe, a small town in the Bombay Hills of New Zealand's North Island.

"He's good company. You don't get lonely if you have someone," says Irene, sipping her tea. "He's a good worker and he helps out quite a bit." She attends the workshop each day to do "fancy work", and Hoppy (a nickname Gene was given in the institution, probably after a stroke which left him with an uneven gait) works at a recyclery.*

Hoppy: We was in King's Seat first and then Raventhorpe. We was in there a long time.

Irene: King's Seat, that's where we first met. We been together ever since. Quite a few of them went to Raventhorpe. They asked us if we wanted to go.

Hoppy: (nods somberly, holding his tea cup on his knee) They ask us.

Irene: They was closing Raventhorpe down then, they was. John, he was our friend, he come with us.

---

*   *A paper recycling center.*

Hoppy: Then we went to a house.

Irene: John and David was with us. . . .

Hoppy: (nods) Gary.

Irene: Gary was with us. We was packed. Could hardly move. I had a room, but it was too many. They thought it would be better if we live together, Hoppy and me. He's a good worker, you know. He helps me out quite a bit. He mows the lawn.

Hoppy: Yes.

Irene: (chews a biscuit, vigorously brushes crumbs from her lap) We never fight. We get on real good. He helps with cookin' and gettin' tea on every night. He turns on the stove.

Hoppy: (holds up his thick fingers, makes the motions for his job) I work at the recyclery. I do the phone books. Cut them off. Take the paper off, too. From the phone books. Cut 'em with the . . . guillotine. Press the button. Push up to the red line. Tight. Push button. Chuck cardboard in the trolley. The paper goes for chicken beds. On the farms. And to pack up flowers.

Irene: I go to the workshop. Do different things. Fancy work. Painting. Knit.

Hoppy: (smiles, raises bushy eyebrows) I like her all right.

Irene: Go on, tell 'er why you like me then.

Hoppy: I seen her in 21.

Irene: (leans forward, whispers) That was a big pen where they put you if you was bad. It's not closed down yet. It should do.

  We used to meet up at the canteen. Then we could see each other. We was in Raventhorpe a long time, wasn't we? We used to go to dances together, didn't we? We used to play Housie.* They had numbers and they used to call out numbers.

Hoppy: (holds a hand in the air) They had cards with numbers and you had to put a button on the number.

Irene: We don't have nothin' like that no more. We miss it. He plays bowls. He won lots of prizes, too. He's got a trophy and a dish. He won socks and everything.

Hoppy: She take care of me. My name is Gene. They call me Hoppy. It's a . . . nickname.

Irene: He plays bowls most every Wednesday night with 'is mates. We are not married, no. He said he doesn't have enough money to get rings. There's a fellow at the workshop who always says to me he says "How's the marriage goin'?" He's always havin' me on, he is. We live together, that's all. We do, don't we? We go out some-times. Sometimes they bring a van. We both walk to the workshop, don't we? Then he goes on from there to work.

---

*   *Bingo equivalent.*

Hoppy: Get up half past six.

Irene: One morning, he almost slept too long, didn't you?

Hoppy: I was born in Russell, but there . . . 1920, about that.

Irene: I'm 59. He's 68. He took me out for tea, didn't you, on my birthday. We went to a lovely chicken place for tea.

You don't get lonely when you have a mate. We don't, do we? We watch TV.

Hoppy: We watch TV.

Irene: That's what we do in the evening, watch the telly, don't we? And sometimes, he gets pickled with beer with his mates, he does. It's really funny!

Hoppy: I like the red one. A lion on it. I like different ones, too, but I like Lion's Beer.

Irene: I fancy a shandy.

Hoppy: You put lemonade in first, then you put beer on top.

Irene: That's right. I've had it plenty of times, haven't I? I don't get pickled though, not like him!

Hoppy: Sometimes we fight.

Irene: Only when he doesn't want to get up to go to work. One morning, I called him and he didn't want to get up so he missed the van. We each have our own room. But I can still hear him snore, can't I?

Hoppy: (smiles slowly) She snores sometimes.

Irene: Raventhorpe was big, it was. Very big. It was packed. One time, he went out shopping with a staff and they came back to Raventhorpe and they was pickled. I had to stay out of his reach, I'll tell you! It was funny. I had sun cancer. I've had it on me leg one time. (Lifts her dress) They took a piece up here on me leg and sewed it on down here. I wear a hat outside in the sun. I got to be careful. He does, too, but he peels sometimes right on the top of his head!

We got a cat.

Hoppy: (nods) Benny. A cat.

Irene: He always goes over to the neighbors, Benny does. He's all fixed up so he can't have any cats. The people who own this house didn't want us to have a cat at first, they don't like cats, but the staff talk them into lettin' us keep Benny. One of the staff at the workshop gave him to us.

Sometimes we go out to shows. They got all different acts, like horses jumping and once there was white rabbits. It was a good show. At the workshop, I make fancy work and we sell them to people what buy them.

He can fix anything if anything gets broken. So he's very handy. He's good to have around so I don't get frightened. Some kids were bothering us for awhile, but we told the police.

Sometimes on a Sunday night I go up to the shops and buy him something so he gets a surprise. Sometimes we go to DEKA, that's a good store. Fifteen dollars to get me hair cut. Fancy spendin' that much money on this old hair!

We do our housework every day, we do. See that frame on the wall? Those pictures in that frame came from the store. We don't know who they are, those people, do we?

We'd rather do things for ourselves. We got our freedom here. We don't have to ask for everything.

Hoppy: (shakes his head) No, we don't.

Irene: (offers a tray of biscuits to him) I got a friend who doesn't have nobody. She gets very sad, don't she? She don't have nobody to look after her, nobody to talk to. He goes to bowls at 7 and walks home again at 9. He don't drink no beer then, when he's got to walk home, do you?

Hoppy: You roll the ball up and try to get in near the middle.

Irene: He's quite good at bowls, he is. He wins prizes. He won tins of fruit and icing sugar. I never know what he's goin' to come home with. But he always comes home, he does.

Beverley Farrell and Trevor Waite

Onehunga, New Zealand

*I*n the older suburban Auckland neighborhood of Onehunga within sight of the city's historic One Tree Hill is a small brick flat that features a scrawl of gang graffiti on its exterior. It is a home owned by the New Zealand Society for the Intellectually Handicapped (IHC). Inside, the living room carries a distinct odor of a cat litter box that has been full for a little too long. Trevor, 32, perches on the edge of a worn easychair, hands clasped over his knees. He is dressed nattily in a shirt and pullover, pressed grey slacks and black shoes.

Bev, 30, looking worried, draws her bare feet under her full blue skirt and pulls down her orange t-shirt. As Trevor talks, almost non-stop, Bev, born in 1963, slowly twirls a strand of hair on one finger and nervously sucks her thumb. Occasionally, she wants to speak and says pleadingly, "Shut up, Trev." Almost startled by her own voice, she remembers her manners and smiles; it is a smile that lights her face and transforms a nervous girl to an attractive woman. "Shut up, Trevor. *Please.*" She beams triumphantly at their IHC support worker, who helps the couple with their weekly budgeting and who is on hand for the interview.

They agree the cat, Sissy, should go outside, but they were devastated when their first cat was run over on the street. Bev cried for weeks. "Beverley gets upset sometimes, she does," says Trevor, born in 1961. Her family does not favor the couple's wish to marry and Bev, despite Trevor's pleading, won't defy them. Trevor insists their relationship will not be complete unless he can "marry Beverley and take her on a proper trip. You know, a honeymoon like. I know Beverley's a backwards girl, but she's a good girl and I love her. And I love her family and I would like them to love me like a son. I'll look after my Beverley, I will."

Trevor: See what we do is, before we met, we didn't know each other. We have a very lovely house here, we do, Bev and me. Margaret comes in and helps us budget. She sees what we need to buy and she helps us do that. We'd like to get a new TV, so I'm going to take Margaret down to the secondhand shop and show it to her, a good one, it is. She's really good to us, Margaret is. We love her.

See when I first met Beverley, this lady called Carolyn introduced me to this girl. She brought her in to where I used to live and I thought she was a very nice girl, I did. I showed her around even when the others didn't like her so much. When we started to be friends slowly and slowly, then we started slowly, didn't we, Bev? But I got booted out of where I used to live. It wasn't Bev's fault, it wasn't. But what they did was they separated us because they didn't like our relationship. We had a meeting. What was it about, Bev?

Beverley: (lowers her eyes) Now don't be embarrassed, Trev. But see I don't want to have no kids. I wanted to have somethin' done. So Trev had somethin' done instead. His family blame me for it, so they split us up.

Trevor: It wasn't cause of Bev. I got very upset bein' split up and someone had to come over straight away and stop me. They had take somethin' off me straight away cause I was so upset I lost Beverley.

Beverley: A knife. My family didn't want us together. They always tell me what to do and I just say to them "Just leave me and Trevor alone." I don't want them to hit me either.

Trevor: We want to get married. Right. This is the hardest part. Bev's family come in the house and in Bev and me's life and tell us we can't get married. The only thing we have problems with is we can't talk with Bev's family. We need someone to come with us. My family is proud of me and Bev bein' together. They love Bev as a daughter. Me mum loves Bev a lot because she gives me mother a hard time, eh, Bev?

    What I'd like to exactly do is put it this way, if Bev wasn't allowed to get married by the family, I should be able to choose who I get married to. But I don't want to upset Beverly cause it's not Bev's fault, eh, Bev. I love Bev a lot. I would never lose Beverly. I know she can do her housework, cookin' on her own, all that. She had trouble with the washing, but she's gettin' good at it. She can hang clothes up. But I tell her it's stupid if you can't get married cause you're over 21. I says if Bev can't get married, why should we live in a relationship? It's hard.

Beverley: My family is not talkin' to me at the moment. . . .

Trevor: It's not Beverley's fault. . . .

Beverley: (frowns and snaps) Shut up for a moment, Trev. Shut up, *please*, I mean. My mum and dad are not talkin' to me.

Trevor: She's scared of them.

Beverley: I'm scared of them. I get whacked.

Trevor: But they're good to us. I really like them a lot like a son, I do. But what I get wild at is when they come here; what I get wild about and angry and they think we're not doin' our best with the housework. But what we do is every Saturday, we get up and do all our cleanin' cause we like to keep this house clean in case the manager comes.

I like Bev's mum and dad and I'd like to try and make Bev's dad happy. He's been sick, but my point is Bev should be allowed to get married cause she's over 21, she is. We've been together so long now we think somethin' should be done. We don't want to hurt Mr. Farrell or Mrs. Farrell, but I do like them a lot.

Bev and I don't go to church. But I would like to go to church, I would. It would help me and Bev get out more. When we go out, like what we do if we haven't got the money to go out, we stay home if we've got no money. If we got money, then I say to Bev "Come on, let's go up to Warlow." If we do buy anything, we always remember to save the dockets* for Margaret so she knows what we spent some money on, eh, Bev?

I really enjoy havin' Beverley with me cause she's good company. We go out. We dance. She's good company. I buy her things for her birthday. We have great fun. We go out and play cards at night. We don't like to use up our bus tickets too much, though. We get on well together and we never fight. If we have an argument, we sit down and sort it out. Anyways, I would never hit a girl cause I like her too much. I was so upset when we was split up and before that I wanted to kill meself and didn't want to see anybody. Then Bev rang me up on the phone and I was so happy, I was smilin' and dancin'.

Beverley: (smiles, smooths her skirt) I thought he was kind of cute. I was very unhappy when my parents broke us up. People were very nasty to me so I said, "Right, I can't be bothered with livin' here anymore" so I wanted to move in with Trevor. I was by myself. . . .

Trevor: Tell what happened when you were alone.

Beverley: Somebody tried to break in. I was very scared. Somebody tried to get me. I rang up Trevor.

Trevor: I was in bed and I got up and walked all the way over. We packed up her clothes and she came over to stay with me and she didn't want to go back to the other place no more.

---

* *Sales receipts.*

Beverley: There was this guy who tried to make me pregnant and he even told Trevor to do things nasty to me, but Trev didn't want to do it. Trev was a gentleman.

Trevor: Wasn't that nice, Bev? She got raped once, she did, by a taxi driver.

Beverley: Oh, yeah. This taxi driver pick me up at where I work, the work school, and I said "Now you take me straight home," but he didn't. He drove me way up to the hill way away from anywhere.

Trevor: (shakes his head) That's shocking.

Beverley: I came home cryin' and I asked my mum to ring the police. They came and took me up there and I didn't want to go. The taxi driver got in trouble for it and his wife blame me for it. I can talk to Trev about things like that. Sometimes he is a good listener. Sometimes he doesn't.

Trevor: We're both good workers. I like to write down on a piece of paper what our chores are. Like every fortnight, we get a whole pile of washin' and we go through if we got any holey socks or clothes that is no good and we chuck them out. It's important to look nice. We're really good and independent. If we get stuck, we know what to do and who to ring up.

If Bev's mum and dad was to sit down with us, I would say "Right." I wouldn't yell at them, I would say to them "Look your other kids are married and you'd better give Beverly a chance." She's 38 and she's much older than me. I'm over 31. I don't know why they're stoppin' her to get married for, but I don't think that's right. If you're over 21, surely you should be able to get married. But I don't take it out on Beverley. She's a lovely girl and I like her too much for that. I know she's backwards, she's a backwards girl and she can't write but she can't help that. I write the grocery list for her.

If she's old enough and is livin' in a relationship, then she should be able to get married. Like all the Auckland ones in the IHC, they get married. I reckon you have every proof to do it. They're not mad from us livin' together, but they just say "Why do you want to get married for?" I was to make Bev happy and take her on a proper holiday. I know she wants to get married. I care about Mr. and Mrs. Farrell. They're part of my family and I want to stick with them and I'd like to tell Mr. Farrell I can look after his daughter, I will. Someone should help us tell him that.

If we was to get married, I would ring up Margaret and ask her if she had some time if she could help me buy a nice suit. She could tell me how much money I had in my account and if I didn't have enough, we could sort somethin' out. If I got married, I would go for a nice brown suit. A nice brown color, eh, Bev?

Beverley: (smiles, picks up the hem of her skirt with two fingers) I would have a white dress. A short white dress.

Trevor: When I first met Beverley, I didn't know what this girl was going to be like. What if this girl was goin' to get married to me? I thought she was a nice person. I was the only one that was nice to her. She's backwards, but I don't blame her that she's backwards. That was the way she's born and she can't help the way she is. Say someone walk in and say "This girl's an IHC girl," I would go over to him and say she can't help it the way she's born. It's the way she is. You wouldn't like that if someone called you that.

We been together, cor, how long? Three years, eh, Bev?

Beverley: Three years, Trev.

Trevor: Next year, it'll be, let's see, four years.

Beverley: Four years.

Trevor: See, we don't want kids. We'd just rather be on our own. I had an operation. My family got upset about that, but it wasn't their choice. It was my choice. I wanted to have that. Before the operation, we went to family plannin' and we decided we didn't want kids cause we know Bev isn't capable of havin' kids. We just want to be our own and have a cat. We are happy with each other. Kids are hard to look after. First you got to have a permanit job so you got enough money. Kids are very dear, you know, they cost a lot of money. We are happy with our decision. You got to bath them when they're small. You got to get them school clothes and get them off to school and if the girl is at work, the man should be at home waitin' for the kids after school and that. You got to feed them. You got to take them to the doctor. We don't want kids. Our cat is just lovely to have. She sleeps during the day. She's lovely.

Beverley: Lovely. I love her.

Trevor: (proudly) Beverley is doing very well, eh, Bev? She knows how to look after herself. She knows how to wash and she knows how to shower and I don't ever have to help her. She cooks a bit, but I'm a better cook, but I don't help her. I just watch. I know how to cook potatoes. When it's her turn, I tell her "It's your turn to cook tea, so go ahead and do it." Then I just turn on the TV and put me feet up!

We love each other, Bev and me do. What we do at night and everything, well, it's kind of embarrassing to talk about (looks at Bev and nods). But what we do is we took things slowly, slowly. What we do is we don't hurt each other. We take things slowly. Very slowly.

(Brightly, after a silence) When you get married, it's good because I reckon when you get married because what I get worried about is that if we don't get married, I'm afraid that someone might take advantage of Beverley. I don't want to lose Bev. I'd like to take her somewhere on a little holiday and if I got married, it just might be a lot better. We want to live our lives and stand up on our own two feet and we would be more settled down if we was married. We are adults. We are not children and we got to act like adults and people don't need to always come into our house and tell us what to do.

Beverley: (twists a strand of hair, glances at Trevor) Mum and Dad don't want me to get married, Trev, because they are waiting for me to learn more skills. They ask me why I want to get married.

Trevor: They ask her, but they don't ask me. They ask her cause she is the daughter of their family.

Beverley: I don't want to hurt them, me mum and dad.

Trevor: Okay, so what if your parents was to . . .

Beverley: (frowns, waves her hand) Shut up, Trev. I mean, shut up *please*, Trev. Don't push me.

Trevor: No, I'm not pushin' (shrugs). See, this is what happens. She is very scared. One time I took Beverley to McDonald's for tea. I surprise her. Bev's really okay.

Beverley: I'd like to learn how to cook more things and do the shoppin'. Money skills are hard.

Trevor: Never mind, Bev. I'll look after you. At least we're doin' well. Our family knows we don't earn much and they feel sorry for us. Sometimes they shout us* to the pools, you know, pay our way. Sometimes when the family shouts you out, I feel so guilty because they feel so sorry for us. But never mind. I'd like to pay them back.

Beverley: It's not fair other people shout us.

Trevor: It's not fair, but at least they love us too much. We'd like to buy some nice things at some nice secondhand shops, you know, some nice things for our house so the colors match in our house. (Surveys the living room, straightens his collar) We'd like to make our house nice. I'd like to make it nice for me and Beverley. I love her and I will take care of her forever.

---

*   *To treat, pay someone's way.*

Marianne Porter and James Richardson

Christchurch, New Zealand

S he carefully signs the interview permission form "Marianne and James Richardson," even though they are not married. Engaged since Christmas Day 1989, Marianne Porter and James, both 39, live together in their Sawyers Arms Road flat. Three other such flats owned by the Society for the Intellectually Handicapped in Christchurch on the same property are occupied by other couples. Theirs is a clean, tidy home and the small living room features his extensive country and western music collection. Marianne works at the Kilmarnock Enterprises cafe: "I help with lunches."

James, born in Dunedin, is a self-described "workin' man" who "likes to have a beer with me mates." He cleans kennels at a nearby dog shelter. "A right honest job," he says. IHC staff occasionally wondered if James preferred the company of men, but agree he's happy with Marianne. He sneaks up on her through the clothes she is hanging on the line outside their flat. Tickling her until she begs him to stop, he kisses her

and repeatedly assures her, his arm firmly around her
shoulders, "We ain't got no worries!"

Marianne: We've been engaged since 1989. Have a few arguments, but we get over them.

James: (stands in the kitchen, hands in his pockets) We argue
sometimes, that's right. Sometimes when I have a bad day at work, I
come home feelin' a bit crook.* But we got no problems, her and
me.

Marianne: It wasn't love at first sight, it wasn't. He was a bit shy.
I was with another man before, but he was a proper jerk.

James: I was just with one girl in me life before. Then I had two.

Marianne: (smiles) And I didn't like her. It was finally between
her and me and I won. I reckon he has a good sense of humour. He
can do lovely Donald Duck impressions. He makes my family
laugh. He's a happy man. I felt a bit sorry for him, with no brothers
and sisters. But when he met my family, I was a bit nervous takin'
him over for tea, but I reckon they like him. I lived at Lake
Coleridge, Canterbury Plains for years until Dad was killed on his
boat. Me and Mum moved to Christchurch and when she died in
1986, my sister helped me join the IHC. Then I met James. Some-

---

*   *Ill.*

times he makes me laugh so I feel I have to go to the toilet in a hurry! Sometimes he makes me laugh so hard I nearly wet meself!

James: I reckon she's ace, Number One! We got no problems. I like country and western tapes, got 350 in that box (waves toward the living room). Tex Morton, Johnny Horton, Slim Dusty . . .

Marianne: We joined the Working Men's Club, it's sort of like a pub where people get together. We walk up the road here.

James: Women can get in, no problem. It's not very far. I drink Canterbury Bitter. That's what I got me this belly from. Yes, I like my beer. Very fond of it. I like Lion's Red, too. Got me a good job at the dog pound, I do. Christchurch Dog Pound. I wash the kennels down.

Marianne: Sometimes he comes home itchy. We've got two cats, that's enough for us. One's called Beatnik and one's called Pudge. She's a wee fatty, she is. Whatever she finds, she eats!

James: We got no hassles, me and Marianne. Sometimes I help her around the house.

Marianne: Sometimes he goes out with his mates early in the morning while I get the housework done. Just gives me a break. Then we do the shopping together.

James smokes his cigarettes. But he does it outside because the smoke gets into my chest.

We each have a bedroom. We have some privacy at least. He's romantic sometimes, he can be. He brings me things for my birthday. He's easy to please anyway. I just get a country and western tape. He doesn't mind.

James: (paces in the kitchen) I enter raffles. I'm quite lucky, aren't I, Marianne? I won a toaster. And meat. My luck is changing. I won two hams last Christmas. We have a provisions account* in a book. No, we got no hassles.

I can't sleep in in the morning. The missuz here can sleep in. Not me. Even when I got me a hangover, you know, the brews blues, I got to get up.

Marianne: We been together four years. We spoke to the family to see if they minded if we move in together. They agreed, so we did. And IHC was on our side all the way. It's sad to see people with disables, you know, they've got something wrong with them and they got no one to live with. No one to visit them. Makes me sad. I feel quite sorry for them. They're worse off than us.

James: She can't have any kids, Marianne can't.

Marianne: Had my tubes tied. Kids are too much hassle anyways. I'd rather be out workin'. I work at Kilmarnock cafe, makin' lunches.

James: Never wanted kids.

---

* *A bank account for groceries and household neccessities.*

Marianne: I like kids, but to have one screamin' and yellin' at night, no. I wouldn't like that. The cats are fine for us!

    Sometimes we fight, him and I. But I usually go for a wee walk down the road, sit in the park here. He comes round about ten minutes later and he's sorry. I yell, then I go for a walk!

James: I treat her like a woman. Buy her anything she wants. Treat her like a woman then, don't I?

Marianne: (pats his arm) You do good. He's good to go with. He's quite cute sometimes. He can be, if he wants to. We went to America once on a trip with the IHC. It's a different day there, you know, and they drive on the wrong side of the road! I'd like to go to Canada one day; I have an auntie in Vancouver. I'll have to save big bickies for that. Maybe win the lotto!

    He gave me my ring on Christmas Day 1989. He got down on one knee, in front of the whole family. We never had a video though.

James: I like my beer, I do. I can't remember what I said. I was half-packed. I think I'll step out for a cigarette, if you don't mind.

Marianne: (shoos him away) Go on, then. He woke up the next morning and said, "Did I get engaged to you? I can't remember!" And I said yes, you did! I thought the beer might have gone to his knees, that's why he got down on one of them! We don't know when we'll get married. We will one day, I suppose, but this is just like it, isn't it? When we do get married, I'll wear white. I don't care how much it costs, but I'll put some of my pay by. My sister got married with a JP and everyone brought a plate, so it was cheap for her. Sensible, I reckon.

I think I'm pretty lucky in a way. My sister tells me "Just don't push your luck when you're arguin'. You might lose him," she says. "Don't push him," she says. That's why I let him go his own way with his mates. And I go with my mates sometimes to the pictures if I feel like it. If I don't feel like it, I just stay here. There's always ironing to do.

There are places I remember
All my life though some have changed.
Some forever, not for better;
Some have gone and some remain.
All these places have their moments
With lovers and friends,
I still can recall.
Some are dead and some are living;
In my life, I've loved them all.
—"In My Life"
John Lennon/Paul McCartney

Afterword

When I was 19, I travelled halfway around the world to live with a New Zealand farm family I had never met. As we lived and worked together during the months that followed, intimate and unique friendships took hold and grew.

Just over thirteen years later, during the writing of this book, I found myself once more on a plane landing at the Auckland International Airport, this time with my husband. My Kiwi friends Paul and Daphne, their kids, and I had kept in touch with letters and photographs over the years, but there was the uncertainty that these were perhaps people I had known very well for a short time a long time ago. Would it be the same? But there are connections that, if we are lucky, endure time and distance. I was welcomed back literally with open arms, instantly at home again with their wonderful accent and euphemisms, with Paul's strong opinions and wry humor, Daphne's gentle and steadfast spirit, and a farm life in a beautiful country that had been my daily routine so many years before. Eight- and ten-year-old Glen and Paula had grown into tall, self-assured, and happy adults; Glen's twin, Brent, had gone off to make his own path in the world. The 13-year interim melted away in the laughter as tales were recounted, launched with "Do you remember when . . .?" A deeper interest in one another's lives was an added pleasure, a dimension only the passage of time can bring.

Each friendship is as distinct and separate as fingerprints (Perske, 1993) and going home again brought with it the realization that I treasure and depend on my far-away New Zealand friends much as I do the people close to me every day. Knowing we think of one another from time to time and that there is a place halfway around the world where I can still feel at home never fails to lift my heart.

I suppose I tell that story because the experience gave me pause
to appreciate the other bonds in my life: with my husband, each of
my three stepchildren, my parents, my brother and his family, my in-
laws—and my array of friends. Each of these connections fulfil and
nurture me in different ways. All are threads—each unique in tex-
ture and hue—woven through me. To lose one is to unravel part of
myself. It is the colorful, comfortable, unpredictable, and sometimes
unexplainable connections with others which make up the ever-
evolving individual. All this "thirtysomething" retrospection also
crystallized the words of the couples I interviewed for this book.
The people who are the happiest, most hardy, and optimistic are
those not only with a partner (and, for some, family), but those with
friends—and many different kinds of them. Not all the people in
this book are "couples" in the sense of having a sexual relationship.
A few are Platonic friends; Hoppy and Irene are as important to one
another as are Phil and Wendy. Even when she's with "a boy who
makes me feel like a girlfriend," 18-year-old Ellen Gajewski's
dream romance with a movie actor fuels her determination to one
day go to New York City. All 15 relationships in *Couples* are different, just as are the circumstances and the people themselves. But
each is a celebrated connection, a freedom to be intimate with
another person, a defense against loneliness, a chance to take care of
and be cared for.

The saddest stories come as quiet longings from people who
find themselves isolated, protected by family or staff from the risks
of daily life, guarded from the risk of exploitation, denied their
sexuality, or simply not encouraged or supported to make friends because that category doesn't appear on an Individual Program Plan. It

is difficult to think that for many people, loneliness is endured every day for a lifetime.

In the living room of their flat, Irene, 59, sat next to Hoppy, 68, the man who's been her closest friend for over 40 years. Staff made sure Hoppy and Irene left the institution together because it was clear they were friends. Sounds simple enough, but too often lifelong friends are torn apart during moves from institutions or group homes. Men and women with disabilities are kept apart and their love is denied, or connections simply forgotten, creating wounds that may never heal (Melberg Schwier, 1993). But today, Hoppy and Irene complain of each other's snoring and nod in unison that living together, even Platonically, is "good company." Irene speaks sorrowfully of a friend who ". . . gets very sad. Hoppy and me, we take care of each other. She don't have nobody. She don't have nobody to care about her or to look after. That's sad, it is."

To many people in this book, one of the most important aspects of their relationship is the chance to take care of someone else. Even a simple friendship calls on each person to see beyond themselves, urges them to contribute to the happiness and growth of another. At the same time, friendships, relationships, attractions are all undefinable things. Relationships do not often lend themselves well to analytical scrutiny. We should be content to know they may be the very heart of community. The beauty of such connections often simply lies in the fact they occur, exist, evolve, sometimes fade away. Sometimes, if we are very lucky, they last a lifetime.

— **K.M.S.**
Saskatoon, Saskatchewan
April 1994

And here is my secret, a very simple secret:
It is only with the heart that one can see
rightly; what is essential is invisible to the eye.
— *The Fox,*
The Little Prince
Antoine de Saint-Exupery

References

Berkobien, R. (1992), Assistant Director, Department of Research and Program Services, The Arc, Arlington, TX. Personal correspondence.

Endicott, O. (1993). Legal counsel, Ontario Association for Community Living, Toronto, Ontario. Personal conversations.

Hasbury, Dave. (1988). Frontier College, Toronto, Ontario. Personal conversations.

Hingsburger, D. (1991). *I Contact: Sexuality and People with Developmental Disabilities*. Mountville, PA: VIDA Publishing.

Hingsburger, D. (1993), I Contact: Education and Consulting, BM 272, 33 des Floralies, Eastman, Quebec. Personal conversations.

Kempton, W. (1988). *Speaking of Sex and Persons with Special Needs*. Videotape interview with James Stanfield. Santa Monica: James Stanfield Publishing.

Kieft, J. (1993), Editor, *Community Moves,* New Zealand Society for the Intellectually Handicapped (IHC), Christchurch, New Zealand. Personal conversations and correspondence.

Kushner, Harold. (1986). In "Why I Am Not Afraid to Die," *When All You've Ever Wanted Isn't Enough: The Search for a Life That Matters*. © by Kushner Enterprises, Inc. New York: Simon & Schuster, Inc.

Melberg Schwier, K. (1993). Ordinary Miracles: Testimonies of Friendships. In A.N. Amado, *Friendships and Community Connections between People with and without Disabilities*. (pp. 155–167). Baltimore: Paul H. Brookes Publishing.

Melberg Schwier, K. (1990). *Speakeasy: People with Mental Handicaps Talk about Their Lives in Institutions and in the Community*. Austin: Pro Ed.

Perske, R. (1993), Introduction. In A.N. Amado, *Friendships and Community Connections between People with and without Disabilities*. (pp. 1–6). Baltimore: Paul H. Brookes Publishing.

Peterson, E. (1988). "Restoring Hope, Dignity Takes Co-ordinated Effort" by K. Melberg in *Dialect*, magazine (Feb. issue). Saskatoon: Saskatchewan Association for Community Living.

Robertson, D. (1991), Presentation at "And Justice for All" Conference on Community, Ellensburg, WA.

Smith, D. (1985). *Minds Made Feeble: The Myth and Legacy of the Kallikaks*. Austin: Pro Ed.

Stehle, B. (1985). *Incurably Romantic*. Philadelphia: Temple University Press.

Terkel, S. (1967). *Division Street: America*. New York: Pantheon Books.

Terkel, S. (1972). *Working: People Talk about What They Do All Day and How They Feel about What They Do*. New York: Pantheon Books.

Wertham, F. (1978), Cited in Wolfensberger, W. "The Extermination of Handicapped People in World War II Germany," *Mental Retardation*, 19(1), 1981.

Recommended Resources

Books

Being Sexual: An Illustrated Sex Education Series for Developmentally Handicapped People. East York, ON: Sex Information & Education Council of Canada (SIECCAN), 1992.*

Colley, L. and Linda Howden. *Facts of Life and Living: A Curriculum That Promotes Social and Sexual Awareness for Persons with Developmental Disabilities*. St. Catharines, ON: Facts of Life and Living, 1991.

Edwards, J.P. and T.E. Elkins. *Just Between Us: A Social Sexual Training Guide for Parents and Professionals Who Have Concerns for Persons with Mental Retardation*. Portland, OR: Ednick Communications, 1988.

Griffiths, D. and D. Hingsburger. *Changing Inappropriate Sexual Behavior: A Community Based Approach for Persons with Developmental Disabilities*. Baltimore, MD: Paul H. Brookes, 1989.

Hingsburger, D. and Susan Ludwig. *Being Sexual: An Illustrated Series on Sexuality and Relationships*. East York, Ontario: The Sex Information and Education Council of Canada, 1993.

Hingsburger, D. *I Contact: Sexuality and People with Developmental Disabilities*. Mountville, PA: VIDA Publishing, 1991.

---

*   *Contains multimedia instructional materials.*

Hingsburger, D. *I Openers: Parents Ask Questions about Sexuality and Their Children with Developmental Disabilities*. Vancouver: Family Support Institute Press, 1993.

Hutchison, P. *Making Friends: Developing Relationships between People with a Disability and Other Members of the Community*. North York, ON: Roeher Institute, 1990.

Kramer Monat-Haller, R. *Understanding and Expressing Sexuality: Responsible Choices for Individuals with Developmental Disabilities*. Baltimore, MD: Paul H. Brookes Publishing, 1992.

Kempton, W. and M.S. Bass, S. Gordon (eds). *Love, Sex, and Birth Control for Mentally Handicapped People: A Guide for Parents*. Philadelphia, PA: Planned Parenthood, 1985.

Kroll, K. and E.L. Klein. *Enabling Romance: A Guide to Love, Sex, and Relationships for the Disabled (and the People Who Care about Them)*. New York, NY: Harmony Books, 1992.

Learning to Love: A Set of Simple Booklets on Sexuality (Contraception, From Child to Adult, How a Baby Is Born, Sex and Making Love and *Health and Infections*). Birmingham, England: Brook Advisory Centres, 1991.

Let's Talk About AIDS. Vancouver, B.C.: The B.C. Coalition of People with Disabilities, 1993.

Let's Talk About Condoms. Vancouver, B.C.: The B.C. Coalition of People with Disabilities, 1993.

Ludwig, S. and D. Hingsburger. *Being Sexual: An Illustrated Series on Sexuality and Relationships for People with Disabilities*. East York, ON: SIECCAN (Sex Information & Education Council of Canada), 1992.

Mathews, Jay. *A Mother's Touch: The Tiffany Callo Story*. New York, NY: Henry Holt and Company, 1992.

McKee, L. et al. *An Easy Guide to Loving Carefully for Men and Women*. Walnut Creek, CA: Planned Parenthood, 1987.

Maksym, D. *Shared Feelings: A Parent's Guide to Sexuality Education for Children, Adolescents, and Adults Who Have a Mental Handicap*. North York, ON: Roeher Institute, 1990.

Meyers, R. *Like Normal People*. London: Souvenir Press, 1979.

Novak Amado, A. (ed) *Friendships and Community Connections between People with and without Developmental Disabilities*. Baltimore, MD: Paul H. Brookes, 1993.

Perske, R. *Circles of Friends: People with Disabilities and Their Friends Enrich the Lives of One Another*. Nashville, TN: Abingdon Press, 1988.

Quackenbush, M. and M. Nelson. *The AIDS Challenge: Prevention Education for Young People*. Santa Cruz, CA: Network Publications, 1988.

Sexual Abuse Prevention Programs and Mental Handicap: A Report Prepared by the G. Allan Roeher Institute. North York, ON: Roeher Institute, 1989.

Schwab, William. *Sexuality in Down Syndrome*. New York, NY: National Down Syndrome Society, 1990.

Shea, V. and B. Gordon. *Growing Up: A Social and Sexual Education Picture Book for Young People with Mental Retardation*. Chapel Hill, NC: Clinical Center for the Study of Development & Learning Library, 1991.

Siegel, P.C. *Changes in You: A Clearly Illustrated, Simply Worded Explanation of the Changes of Puberty for Boys/Girls*. Richmond, VA: Family Life Education Associates, 1991.

Smith, J.D. and K.R. Nelson. *The Sterilization of Carrie Buck*. Far Hills, NJ: New Horizon Press, 1989.

Sobsey, D., Gray, S., Wells, D., Pyper, D. & Reimer-Heck, B. *Disability, Sexuality and Abuse: An Annotated Bibliography*. Baltimore, MD: Paul H. Brookes Publishing Co., 1991.

Stehle, B. *Incurably Romantic*. Philadelphia: Temple University Press, 1985.

The New Our Bodies, Ourselves, Boston Women's Health Book Collective. New York: Simon & Schuster, 1990.

The Right to Control What Happens to Your Body: A Straightforward Guide to Issues of Sexuality and Sexual Abuse. North York, ON: Roeher Institute, 1991.

Vulnerable: Sexual Abuse and People with an Intellectual Handicap. North York, ON: Roeher Institute, 1989.

Chapters, Articles, Information Sheets

Cowdrey, Rob. "A Perspective on Parenting," *Journal on Developmental Disabilities*, Vol. 1, No. 1., 1992. Editor: Ivan Brown, Centre for Health Promotion, University of Toronto, 100 College St., Suite 207, Toronto, ON, M5G 1L5.

Endicott, O. "Can The Law Tell Us Who Is Not the Marrying Kind?" *entourage*, Vol. 7, No. 2. North York, ON: Roeher Institute, 1992.

Hutchison, P. "Double Jeopardy: Women with Disabilities Speak Out about Community And Relationships," *entourage*, Vol. 7, No. 2. North York, ON: Roeher Institute, 1992.

Kempton, W. and E. Kahn. "Sexuality and People with Intellectual Disability: A Historical Perspective." *Sexuality and Disability*, 9, 93–111.

Lutfiyya, Zana M. "Reflections on Relationships between People with Disabilities and Typical People." Syracuse, NY: Centre on Human Policy, 1988.

Marafino, Kathleen. "The Right to Marry for Persons with Mental Retardation," in *When a Parent is Mentally Retarded*, B.Y. Whitman and P.J. Accardo, eds. Baltimore, MD: Paul H. Brookes Publishing, 1990.

"Sexuality and Developmental Disability," regular section, *SIEC-CAN Newsletter*. East York, ON: SIECCAN (Sex Information & Education Council of Canada), 1992.

Walker-Hirsch, L. and M. Champagne. "Circles Revisited: Ten Years Later." *Sexuality and Disability*, 9, 143–148.

Watt, J.W. *Talking Openly about Sexuality*. Presentation at the "And Justice for All" conference, Ellensburg, WA, October 1991.

Video

"Keys of Our Own." Producers Sally Armstrong and Jim Ericson. North York, ON: Roeher Institute, 1993.

"Ready for Love?" Producers *48 Hours*, CBS Television, 1993.
Transcripts and/or videotapes of this segment are available by
writing 48 Hours Transcripts, Box 7, Livingston, New Jersey,
07035, USA. 1–800–338–4847.

Curricula

*AIDS: Training People with Disabilities to Better Protect Them-
selves*. New York, NY: Young Adult Institute, 1987.*

Champagne, M. and L. Walker-Hirsch. *Circles: A Multi-media
Package to Aid in the Development of Appropriate So-
cial/Sexual Behavior in the Developmentally Disabled Individual*. Santa Barbara, CA: James Stanfield Publishing, 1987.*

Champagne, M. and L. Walker-Hirsch. *Circles III: Safer Ways*.
Santa Monica, CA: James Stanfield Publishing, 1990.*

Kempton, W. *Life Horizons*. Santa Barbara, CA: James Stanfield
Publishing, 1988.

Kempton, W. and F. Caparulo. *Sex Education for Persons with Disabilities That Hinder Learning: A Teacher's Guide*. Santa Barbara, CA: James Stanfield Publishing, 1989.*

Livingston, V. and M.E. Knapp. *Human Sexuality: A Portfolio for
Persons with Developmental Disabilities, 2nd ed.* Seattle, WA:
Planned Parenthood, 1991.

---

*   *Contains multimedia instructional materials.*

Ludwig, S. *Sexuality: A Curriculum for Individuals Who Have Difficulty with Traditional Learning Methods*. Newmarket, ON: Community Health Nursing (Regional Municipality of York Public Health), 1989.

Maurer, L. *Positive Approaches: A Sexuality Guide for Teaching Developmentally Disabled Persons*. Wilmington, DE: Planned Parenthood, 1991.

Not a Child Anymore. Birmingham, England: Brook Advisory Centres, 1991.

Siegal, P. *Changes in You: An Introduction to Sexual Education through an Understanding of Puberty*. Santa Barbara, CA: James Stanfield Publishing, 1991.

Simpson, K. (ed). *The Family Education Program Manual*. Walnut Creek, CA: Planned Parenthood, 1990.

Stangle, J. *Special Education: Secondary F.L.A.S.H. (Family Life and Sexual Health: A Curricula for 5th through 10th Grades)*. Seattle, WA: Family Planning Publications (Seattle-King County Dept. of Public Health), 1991.

Journals/Newsletters

abilities, Canada's lifestyle magazine for people with disabilities, Canadian Abilities Foundation, Box 527, Toronto, ON, M5S 2T1.

The Canadian Journal of Human Sexuality. "Sexuality and Developmental Disability" section, Sex Information and Education Council of Canada (SIECCAN), 850 Coxwell Ave., East York, Ontario, M4C 5R1. (416)466–5304.

Community Moves. IHC (The New Zealand Society for the Intellectually Handicapped), National Office, 57 Willis St., P.O. Box 4155, Wellington. (04) 472 2247.

Connections: The Newsletter of the National Center for Youth with Disabilities. NCYD, Box 721, University of Minnesota Hospital & Clinic, Harvard St. at East River Rd., Minneapolis, MN 55455, (800) 333–6293.

entourage. Roeher Institute, Kinsmen Bldg., York Campus, 4700 Keele St., North York, Ontario, M3J 1P3. (416) 661–9611.

Exceptional Parents: Guide for Active Adults with Disabilities. Psy-Ed Corp., 1170 Commonwealth Ave., 3rd Fl., Boston, MA 02134–9942, (800) 852–2884.

Impact. Institute on Community Integration, University of Minnesota, College of Education, 109 Pattee Hall, 150 Pillsbury Dr. S.E., Minneapolis, MN 55455.

It's Okay: Adults Write about Living and Loving with a Disability. Phoenix Counsel, Inc., 1 Springbank Dr., St. Catharines, Ontario, L2S 2K1.

Journal of Sexuality and Disability. Human Sciences Press, Inc., 233 Spring St., New York, NY 10013-1578. (212) 620–8466.

Network Magazine. National Training Resource Centre, Kimberley Centre, Private Bag 4004, Kimberley Rd., Levin, New Zealand. 64 (0) 6 368 7159.

NICHCY: News Digest. National Information Center for Children and Youth with Disabilities, Box 1492, Washington, DC 20013, (202) 416–0300.

Organizations

American Association on Mental Retardation
444 N. Capitol St. NW, Suite 846
Washington, DC 20001–1570
(202) 387–1968
(800) 424–3688
(202) 387–2193 fax

The AAMR is an interdisciplinary association of professionals, parents, consumers, and others interested in intellectual disabilities. The Association offers training and resources on a variety of issues, including sexuality.

The ARC: National Organization on Mental Retardation
500 E. Border St., Suite 300
Arlington, TX 76010
(817) 261–6003
(817) 277–0553 TDD

There are state ARC's nation-wide. The head office will have a complete list available. Programs and projects of The Arc targets a wide range of needs of children and adults who have intellectual disabilities. Services include employment, training, education, independent living, and other supports.

The B.C. Coalition of People with Disabilities
AIDS & Disability Action Project
204–456 W. Broadway
Vancouver, B.C. Canada V5Y 1R3
(604) 875–0188
(800) 663–1278

This organization offers HIV/AIDS educational materials for people with mental handicaps, their families, and support networks. They provide support and information for planning workshops on HIV/AIDS and sexuality for people and offers training kits, workshop outlines, articles, bibliographies, and HIV/AIDS pamphlets.

Canadian Association for Community Living
    and Roeher Institute
Kinsmen Bldg., York Campus
4700 Keele Street
North York, Ontario Canada M3J 1P3
(416) 661–9611

There are provincial and local ACL's nation-wide. The head office will have a complete list available. This is a national federation of advocacy organizations offering a variety of supports and services to people with intellectual disabilities and their families. The Roeher Institute is the research, education, and training wing of CACL.

Canadian Down Syndrome Society
206–12837–76th Ave.
Surrey, B.C. V3W 2V3
(604) 599–6009

The CDSS is a national support organization, offering current information on a wide variety of topics to parents, self-advocates, and various professionals. The Society provides opportunities for people with Down syndrome to express their views and concerns and to participate in the direction of the Society.

Council of Canadians with Disabilities
(formerly COPOH)
926–294 Portage Ave.
Winnipeg, MB R3C 0B9
(204) 947–0303
(204) 942–4625

The CCD is a national advocacy organization of persons with disabilities, with the motto "A Voice of Our Own." It is an organization *of,* not *for,* people with disabilities.

IHC (The New Zealand Society for
the Intellectually Handicapped)
National Office, 57 Willis Street
P.O. Box 4155
Wellington, New Zealand
(04) 472 2247

The IHC advocates for the rights of all people with an intellectual handicap and helps to empower individuals to advocate personally for their rights. The Society offers a variety of programs and services throughout New Zealand. There are branches of IHC throughout the country. The national office will have a complete list available.

National Center for Youth with Disabilities
Univ. of Minnesota, Box 721-UMHC
Harvard St. at East River Rd.
Minneapolis, MN 55455
800–333–6293
(612) 624–3939 TDD

The NCYD is an information and resource center focusing on adolescents with chronic illnesses and disabilities. NCYD maintains the National Resource Library, a comprehensive database of current information about chronic illnesses and disabilities, including learning disabilities.

National Down Syndrome Congress
1605 Chantilly Drive, Suite 250
Atlanta, GA 30324
(404) 633–1555
(1–800–232–NDSC)

The Congress is a national network of parent groups and organizations, serving the needs of families in their local communities. It encourages research, serves as a clearinghouse on information, advises parents on a variety of issues, addresses social policy development, and advocates for the full spectrum of human and civil rights for persons with Down syndrome.

National Down Syndrome Society
666 Broadway, Suite 810
New York, New York 10012
(212) 460–9330
1–800–221–4602

NDSS gets accurate, up-to-date information in English and Spanish on Down syndrome to parents, professionals, and other interested people. An 800 hotline is available at all times so people can receive information, referral to resources throughout the country and answers to questions in a wide variety of issues.

National Fragile X Foundation
1441 York St., Suite 215
Denver, CO 80206
(303) 333–6155
   The foundation provides information about fragile X syndrome, one of the leading genetic causes of intellectual disabilities. It publishes a newsletter, and supports research into diagnosis, treatment, and education of individuals with fragile X.

National Training Resource Centre
Kimberley Centre
Private Bag 4004
Levin (Christchurch), New Zealand
   The Centre exists to promote quality in the lives of people who have intellectual disabilities by increasing the availability of information, training, and education for people involved in human services.

NICHCY: National Information Center for Children
    and Youth with Disabilities
P.O. Box 1492
Washington, DC 20013
(202) 416–0300
(202) 416–0312 fax
   As a national clearinghouse, NICHCY provides information on issues pertaining to children with disabilities. It is devoted to improving the health and social functioning of children with disabilities by providing technical assistance, consultation, and information. Many free publications are available.

People First of Canada
489 College Street, Suite 308
Toronto, ON M6G 1A5
(416) 920–9530
(416) 920–9503 fax

This self-advocacy movement was started by people who had been labelled mentally handicapped. They believed that society had to be told that labels hurt and that they wanted to be known as "people, first." In Canada, the federal organization has eight provincial groups representing over 80 local chapters. Members are making their own decisions, gaining power, and taking control over their lives. The members promote equality for all people who have an intellectual and/or other disability.

Planned Parenthood Federation of Canada
1 Nicholas St., Suite 430
Ottawa, ON K1N 7B7
(613) 238–4474
(613) 238–1162 fax
See below.

Planned Parenthood Federation of America, Inc.
810 Seventh Ave.
New York, NY 10019

Planned Parenthood provides unplanned pregnancy counseling and referrals and education on sexual and reproductive health and family planning. Information services cover issues in pregnancy, prenatal health, fertility, birth control, parenting, human growth and development, social/sexual concerns, and community support services.

Sex Information & Education Council of the U.S. (SIECUS)
130 W. 42nd St., Suite 2500
New York, NY 10036
(212) 819–9770

SIECUS affirms that sexuality is a natural and healthy part of living and advocates the right of individuals to make responsible sexual choices. SIECUS develops, collects, and disseminates information and promotes comprehensive education about sexuality. SIECUS advocates that persons with physical and/or mental disabilities receive sexuality education, sexual health care, and opportunities for socializing and sexual expression.

Sex Information and Education Council of Canada (SIECCAN)
850 Coxwell Ave.
East York, Ontario M4C 5R1 Canada
(416) 466–5304

SIECCAN is a national, non-profit organization established to foster public and professional education about human sexuality. It publishes the *Canadian Journal of Human Sexuality,* which contains a special "Sexuality and Developmental Disability" section. It also publishes the new Blissymbol-translated series entitled *Being Sexual: An Illustrated Series on Sexuality and Relationships.* SIECCAN maintains a unique and extensive resource collection and information service covering the major areas of human sexuality.

Special Needs Project
3463 State St., Suite 282
Santa Barbara, CA 93105
(805) 683–9633
(805) 683–2341

The Project is a resource center and clearinghouse for books about issues relating to physical and mental disabilities aimed at self-advocates, family members, teachers, librarians, and others. A wide range of resources is available on many issues, including sexuality.

TASH: The Association for Persons with Severe Handicaps
11201 Greenwood Ave. N.
Seattle, WA 98133
(206) 361–8870
(206) 361–9208 fax

TASH has available a number of articles and reproductions of pamphlets on the subject of sexuality, photocopies of which are available free of charge. TASH can also refer individuals to several professionals who have offered themselves as human resources on the subject of the sexuality of people with disabilities.

United Cerebral Palsy Association
7 Penn Plaza, Suite 804
New York, NY 10001
(212) 268–6655
(800) USA–1UCP

UCP is an organization for people with cerebral palsy and their families. Through local chapters, it provides a variety of services, including information and referral, parent support, and advocacy. The national association can provide the address of your nearest affiliate.

Young Adult Institute
460 West 34th Street
New York, NY 10001–2382
(212) 563–7474

The YAI is a human and health services agency for people with developmental disabilities, their families, and professionals. With over 90 programs in eight countries, YAI has one of the nation's most diversified and comprehensive community-based residential, clinical, employment, and family support resource networks serving infants, children, adults, and senior citizens. YAI is also nationally renowned for its publications, conferences, training seminars, and television programs which offer information and essential support services.

Parenting Programs

While many view parents with intellectual disabilities as incompetent, thanks to programs such as these and many others, it has been shown that with careful attention and support, many can do well. Contact any of these programs for information.

Dr. Alexander Tymchuk, Director
SHARE/UCLA Parenting Project
Department of Psychiatry
School of Medicine, UCLA
Los Angeles, CA 90024–1759
(310) 825–0026
(310) 206–4446 fax

Dr. Maurice Feldman, Director
Surrey Place Centre
2 Surrey Place
Toronto, Ontario M5S 2C2
(416) 925–5141
(416) 923–8476 fax

Dr. Barbara Whitman, Director
Parents Learning Together
Family Services and Family Studies
Knights of Columbus Developmental Center

Cardinal Glennon Children's Hospital
1465 S. Grand Blvd.
St. Louis, MO 63104
(314) 577–5609

Mary Yoder, Director
Project: Rescue
215 Lakewood Way S.W.
Suite 105
Atlanta, GA 30315

About the Author

Karin Melberg Schwier is a Canadian author and illustrator whose most noted works are about people with intellectual disabilities. Her writing has been recognized with awards from the Canadian Association for Community Living, the U.S. National Down Syndrome Congress, and the Association for Media, Technology and Education in Canada, among others.

Some of her most recent publications include *Keith Edward's Different Day,* an illustrated children's story about individual differences (Impact Publishers, 1992) and *Speakeasy: People with Mental Handicaps Talk about Their Lives in Institutions and in the Community* (PRO ED, 1990). Recent freelance projects include the illustrated children's workbook *Touch the Sky: A Booklet All about Me to Help Me Cope with Cancer* for Candlelighters of Canada.

As the communications coordinator for the Saskatchewan Association for Community Living, an advocacy organization for people with intellectual disabilities in Canada, she produces a provincial magazine, *Dialect.* She has served for several years as a member of the national editorial board of *entourage,* a magazine published by the Canadian Association for Community Living.

Karin Melberg Schwier lives in Saskatoon, Saskatchewan, with her husband, Richard. They have three children, Jim, 20, Erin, 17, and Benjamin, 13.